A Candle
at
Midnight

BY MARCY HEIDISH

A Woman Called Moses
a novel based on the life of Harriet Tubman

The Secret Annie Oakley
a novel based on the legendary sharpshooter

Witnesses
a novel based on the life of Anne Hutchinson

Miracles
a novel based on Mother Seton, first American Saint

Deadline
a novel of suspense

The Torching
a novel of supernatural suspense

A Dangerous Woman
Mother Jones, An Unsung American Heroine
a novel of a self-proclaimed Hell Raiser

ALSO BY MARCY HEIDISH

Who Cares? Simple Ways YOU Can Reach Out

A Candle At Midnight

Soul And The City

*Defiant Daughters: Christian Women of
Conscience*

Keeping Vigil
As a Path Through Depression

A Candle
at
Midnight

By Marcy Heidish

Dolan & Associates

A Candle at Midnight

Printing History
First Printing, 2001, Ave Maria Press, Inc., P.O. Box 428,
Notre Dame, IN 46556. ISBN-10: 0-87793-708-7.

Republication 2009, Dolan & Associates, Publishers
ISBN-13: 978-0-9792404-7-8
ISBN-10: 0-9792404-7-6

Library of Congress Cataloging-in-Publication Data
Heidish, Marcy.
  A candle at midnight : keeping vigil as a path through
  depression /Marcy Heidish.
    p. cm.
  ISBN: 978-0-9831164-6-2
  Includes bibliographical references
Library of Congress Control Number: 2010942513

....

Third edition

FOR MY FATHER

WITH MY LOVE

Contents

ONE

Finding Spiritual
Support in Depression

How do you walk through the valley of the shadow?
Can you navigate if you get lost?
What lights your way?

At some time, all of us pass through life's inevitable
"shadow-lands"—that state of being where everything
seems drained of color and purpose; where "the sun is
always shining somewhere else, over a hill, around a bend
in the road," writes C. S. Lewis. For many, that "somewhere else" is easily reached, soon enough, but for others,
the direction is different, leading into the treacherous
terrain of depression.

Always part of the human experience, depression is
among its most devastating conditions. No culture or era
is exempt, including our own. The anonymous and famous
have been affected alike, from Michelangelo to Abraham
Lincoln to Emily Dickinson. Millions of others who, in
Thoreau's words, lead "lives of quiet desperation" may

also be leading lives of quiet depression, shamed into silence. Long misunderstood, this condition has been seen as self-indulgence, moral weakness, flawed character, insanity, and always, a resounding disgrace.

At last, we are talking more openly about depression, without the stigmatizing language. In fact, the subject is now a timely concern. In December 1999, the Surgeon General made headlines when he issued the first *Report on Mental Health,* a ground-breaking work that shows the stunning national scope of depression.

The importance of integrated medical and psychological approaches was emphasized, and the term "illness" displaced the echo of "madness." These are encouraging signs of progress, with great potential for more, yet something remains unaddressed.

What is missing?

A SPIRITUALITY OF DEPRESSION

Can we treat the body and the mind—but ignore the soul?

A spiritual approach is needed, even demanded, by the very nature of depression, which strikes directly at the core of the self. Our deepest sense of being may be affected, along with our will, outlook, motivation, and spirituality. In major depression, we can feel eclipsed, estranged from life, and, often, utterly abandoned by God. In the midst of our struggle, we may recall, with new meaning, the anguished cry of Jesus from the cross: "My God, my God, why have you forsaken me?"

This sense of alienation from God and from life can deepen, leading to serious consequences. Medical and psychological help are important; without intervention depression worsens. As crucial as these treatments are, however, there is no swift relief. Medication and therapy need time to work. They are powerful allies, but they do not promise what they can't deliver: support for the spirit in the midst of pain, an awareness of God in the dark.

What is needed is a spiritual approach, one that can reach right into the pain and the dark, offering timely comfort and sustained support. It is there while we wait for a therapy session or new medication, during the desert stretches of wakeful nights. Right from the start and all the way, this approach can uphold us, renewing a sense of connection with life and with God. Day by day, a spiritual dimension brings unique forms of strength, solace, and even a flicker of that great fire of far-off hope.

The Power of the Spiritual

The power of the spiritual way is real—not mere dreamy speculation. A significant body of writings, based on solid research and clinical trials, shows that spiritual approaches to medical situations, integrated with other methods, have genuine, positive, measurable effects. There are many examples of such works, such as Dr. Larry Dossey's respected book, *Healing* Words, showing the beneficial alliance of science and prayer.

"Prayer is universal," Dossey writes. "Many people believe that prayer is old-fashioned in our modern scientific age ... [but] scientists studying the effects of prayer have found compelling evidence of the benefits of prayer.... The body appears to *like* prayer and responds...." Experiments with plants and animals disprove a placebo effect, Dossey observes. "One of the most remarkable trends in modern medicine is the return to prayer," he notes, adding that a high proportion of scientists today believe in God and prayer's positive effect on illness.

Prayer does not "discriminate" between forms or phases of illness. In depression these range from mild to major, acute to chronic, reactive (to a situation) to clinical (biochemical). In addition to existing treatment forms, a spiritual approach would benefit all these aspects.

How can *we* make a spiritual approach work?

How would this theory play out in *our* lives?

THE ANCIENT ART OF KEEPING VIGIL

There is an answer—deceptively simple, remarkably strong, reverenced, yet accessible: the ancient Christian tradition of *vigil-keeping*. Passed down through generations, this practice is a time-honored spiritual way to face life's stretches of difficulty, uncertainty, and waiting. A rich custom that has never gone stale, it can help us illuminate the overwhelming experience of depression and renew our sense of God's care for us in the midst of it all.

Vigil-keeping, by its very nature, is an ideal "fit" with the intrinsic nature of depression. Both involve waiting and watching, trust and endurance, and an interplay of light and dark.

A vigil is not a cure, and this is one of its aspects that makes it so right for a depressive illness. There is no promise of a sudden, dramatic turn-around, which might raise unrealistic expectations. A vigil teaches us how to *abide,* trust, and bear with darkness in the presence of God: skills essential to enduring a depression, which seldom moves along as rapidly as we would wish.

The vigil practice does not push us to move faster than we can—to act, to *do.* It allows us simply to *be,* just as we are, and in certain phases of depression, simply *being* is all we can manage. A vigil honors and supports this stage, and in so doing, helps us move on when the timing is right and we are ready.

Time Shaped by Vigils

Vigils provide rhythms that balance the day, center the spirit, and directly address the issue of time. For a depressed person, time is not a minor matter: in the course of this illness, time can flatten and stretch out like a desert, empty and vast and daunting. The day, or the night, becomes something to get through: a sickening dimness, littered with our regrets, rejections, and failures—a space where we feel stuck, useless, and often frightened. What is happening to us? We no longer know. We are, quite literally, lost in time.

A vigil, however, offers a simple, accessible structure for a day that seems vacant, a night that seems endless. Time is arranged around periods of prayer, readings, and reflection. As we pause for these short intervals, we become aware that we are less isolated than we feel. We are, indeed, surrounded by a great cloud of witnesses.

Time-Honored Biblical Vigils

Many others have passed this way before us, and often, in the face of darkness, they kept vigils. The Old Testament presents Jacob keeping watch by the Jabbok river where he finds himself wrestling with a mysterious Being . . . perhaps an angel? The prophet Elijah, despairing in a cave, watches and waits for a sense of God's presence which is not in an earthquake, not in a whirlwind, but in a "still, small voice." This Voice speaks again through the soaring poetry of Ezekiel and Isaiah, luminous with images of hope and comfort for a waiting, sorrowful people.

The vigil theme continues in the New Testament, with the gospels and the Pauline epistles, which urge us to wait and watch for the fullness of God's presence. Moreover, we find that vigils occupy significant places in all four gospels, positioned in the most crucial, climactic situations, at the very core of Christian faith.

There is the unforgettable, agonized night-watch kept by Jesus in the Garden of Gethsemane. Then, as Jesus is taken away and questioned, Peter keeps watch nearby—in a personal vigil of grief after denying his Lord. The faithful women, including the Virgin Mary, keep vigil during the crucifixion; another vigil begins as Jesus lies in the tomb, ending in the joy of the resurrection.

Vigils Light the Church

The young Christian community recalled these vigils of faith and kept their own throughout the first three centuries of persecution, peril, and secret prayer-gatherings. Gradually, liturgical vigils emerged: our seasons of Advent and Lent arose from vigils preceding Christmas and Easter. More vigils emerged around other holy days during the Middle Ages, when the custom was widespread, influenced by monasticism. During the Counter-Reformation, the practice was deepened by such mystics as St. John of the Cross, author of *The Dark Night of the Soul.* Through the centuries, other spiritual writers have enriched personal vigil-keeping, from Julian of Norwich to Thomas Merton.

The vigil tradition helped earlier Christians give shape and meaning to their faith-in-action, faith-under-siege. Vigils also became a way for the community to recall, relive, and honor crucial events in the gospels, often symbolized by light enduring the darkness—a fitting emblem for what Merton calls the "paschal movement" from death to new life.

Vigil as Gift in Depression

Today, the vigil form has much to teach and offer us. We often think of waiting as passive, boring. By contrast, the Christian vigil tradition presents a model of creative, *active* waiting, highly useful to us in depression. Even if we feel isolated, in despair, we are still "in solidarity" with those early vigil-keepers. Throughout this book, we will draw on their witness, experience, and example.

From them, we learn about *active waiting* as a spiritual art and a way through illness.

If we can see our depression as an *actual vigil,* we can reinterpret and perhaps transform an experience that might otherwise render us hopeless, helpless, and defeated. Through the vigil, as we discern where God is for us in depression, we may find unexpected occasions for spiritual growth. A potentially devastating time may instead yield new insight about the heart of our faith, Christ's passion, and because depression renders us so vulnerable, we may slowly lean into God's presence as we have not before. So it has been, gradually, for me.

MY WALK IN THE SHADOWLANDS

These pages emerged from my own experience with clinical depression, which has come and gone through most of my life. In my teens and twenties, frightened and bewildered, I fled this strange "mood," as I thought of it, trying to discount and disown it.

For many years, as an adult, I refused to accept or name this on-and-off condition, even as I became more aware of its presence, and how I had inherited it. I felt as if I carried a secret weakness, a flaw that I could not show anyone, even God.

Traditional therapy helped me in certain ways, but the depression remained untouched. When it wasn't apparent, I still sensed it out there somewhere, like a faceless intruder, waiting silently, edging nearer. When its time came around, I seemed to be caught in a strong, invisible net. However hard I struggled, there was no escaping, and no way I knew to pray through these ordeals, which were unlike any others.

At last, I faced the illness, called it by name, and walked through its valley of the shadow again, this time with my eyes open. I began all over again with a new doctor, a specialist in psychopharmacology who *combines* medications, carefully balanced, if a single drug does not bring results. This sounded hopeful, but I did not anticipate the time, effort, and discouragement involved with this approach. Some drugs made me feel wired or sedated or just plain sick. The longer the process went on, I began to lose hope that anything would help me. Clearly, there was no "magic bullet." I began to dread that I would always be ill.

What More Is Needed?

At this point, I felt a need for something in addition to my existing treatment. First of all, I needed help to stay with the program and reject the temptation to give up. But didn't I have that help already? I was blessed with gifted physicians, loving support at home, and caring friends. What else could I possibly want?

The next week, I walked into my doctor's waiting room and saw a young man curled in the fetal position, asleep on the couch: a study in denims and despair. He looked like the embodiment of a shipwrecked soul, isolated on a raft—alone. Later, at home, I could not get that image out of my mind.

When I next returned to my doctor, the waiting room was empty, except for a pretty, well-dressed woman weeping quietly, steadily, ceaselessly; dangling from her fingers hung a key chain with a small silver heart. Her face was wet. The chain looked fragile. The heart trembled in midair. A chill came over me. This woman, like the sleeping man, looked as if she felt utterly alone. I knew I did too.

A Spiritual Approach to Depression

Depression had isolated each of us, breaking down our sense of connection with the world—and any power other than depression. At times, during my illness, I had been feeling abandoned by God, but there, in that waiting room, I wanted to feel God's hand on my life again; I wanted to sense God's presence in this time, this illness, and with these others in the shadowlands.

A spiritual approach, that was what I needed. Daily, hourly, I needed a way to feel God's care and guidance in the midst of this struggle. Awkwardly, tentatively, I began to grope for some spiritual practice that might fit my state of being. The idea of a vigil began to emerge, perhaps, at first, because I always found meaning in a simple ritual: lighting vigil candles. As a child, I had felt a sense of prayer and presence in this custom: God's abiding care. Now, as an adult, I experimented with various vigil forms and found that they made a striking difference with my depression and, I believe, helped me stick with the rigors of medication trials.

And so I held on. Eventually, my doctor found the right medicinal "cocktail" for my case. The medications began to work and I started—cautiously, warily—to recover.

Vigils for All Seasons

The art of vigil-keeping has stayed with me: an enriching spiritual practice for its own sake, in all seasons. It also helps me deal with the possibility of relapse or recurrence.

My illness may cycle back. With my genetic inheritance and history, this is probable. My father's depression was complex and severe, as was his father's before him. Mine, in a different form, came through the genes and cannot be wished away. For me, such depressive episodes are countered with the right medications, but some of those may lose effectiveness over time. I may need to try new ones—a process worth the struggle but, usually, not an easy time.

Depression is a condition with which I live. It is in remission, controlled, dormant—but never banished. At first, this was devastating, but I came to accept my situation because I have reliable resources to which I can always turn, whatever course my illness may take. My faith is crucial. The art of vigil-keeping will always lead me back to God if I lose my way.

During my last severe depression, the practice of keeping vigil gave me a sense of order and spiritual direction. As I worked out readings and meditations for each day's vigil, my experience of depression began to change. I also felt a sense of gratitude for many small things. Once tangential, they now seemed central: the rich colors in a row of books, a friend's laughter, the smell of old books or a half-peeled orange.

After a depression, the world looks different. Less is taken for granted. Certain things, once important, fade into a new perspective. Vigil-keeping helped to get me to this point, helps me stay there, and sustains me as I look ahead. I like the personal aspect of the vigil, its shape and its balance, the way it frames each day.

Now, I feel acutely aware of others in depression. In my mind, I still see those two patients in the waiting room. I always will. I wanted to write something for those who stand invisibly beyond those people, something of hope. If my experience could be useful to someone who feels as I did, that would be a blessing, a bridge over darkness that we make together, beginning today.

To Keep Vigil Is to Keep Hope

This book is meant to companion you in all the waiting places of depression, in any form, your own or a loved one's. You are invited to explore the art of vigil-keeping:

its history, its practice, and its offerings for you in your own encounters with depression. Through new and ancient prayers, specially chosen readings and rituals, you will discover a way to feel sustained and spiritually nourished by the words of others who have known the intersection of struggle and faith.

As you explore the vigil tradition, I hope you will find a new sense of where God is for you, even in the midst of depression. This book presents you with specially crafted vigils to use according to how you are feeling. You will be invited to create a journal for this process: depression, struggle, and healing. In it, you might track your depression and add your feelings, prayers, and reflections.

This journal, if you choose to keep it, will become a kind of faith story—your story, and if the depression returns, you will be forewarned and forearmed, with a personally crafted journal, record, and guide. In any case, you will be involved in a creative process.

This book is yours to use as you wish. In every case, you are invited to do only as much or as little as feels right for you at the time. No book, including this one, is a substitute for medical care or psychotherapy. Instead, these pages are designed to enhance your treatment, undergirding your entire experience with a spiritual dimension.

Through this exploration, may you find returning hope, slowly, surely, like a ribbon of daylight under a door. May your pain and sense of emptiness recede, and may you hear Christ say to you: "Be not afraid, I go before you always."

■

TWO

Into the Vast Maze:
The Shape of Depression

Rome's Catacombs, 257 A.D.

Quietly, they gathered. Even here, there was a risk. They were watched, their meetings banned. There had been more arrests, more jailed. Always now, as they went about their lives, they listened for soldiers, for mobs; they braced for whippings and the taste of blood. These were troubled times, but they had come before. Their community endured, the faith was kept and witnessed. That was why they gathered here, to worship in the catacombs.

Now, they started down the steps into the vast underground maze. Every time, this felt like a descent to hell. Darkness flooded in around them, cold, black, fluid, like rising water. A single torch, held high, led them to the city of the dead. Twisting, winding, intersecting, all these passageways were lined with tombs. This was no place for the living; few entered the maze except these Christians. On the feast days of the martyrs, they came with vigil lamps and torches for their secret worship. In the light-pricked dark, they prayed the forbidden prayers and sang forbidden hymns. Their *Amens* and *Our Fathers* lingered, sweet and stubborn, on the chilly air. There they stood, these banned believers, lifting up cold hands in praise. There they stood, centered in the lamp light, circled by the dead, cradled by the maze, gathering as one to sing. Their voices, strung together, sounded like a stroked harp: *Alleluia! Christ is risen!* They dreaded the way back. Darkness tricked them. Tunnels coiled around them like a charmer's snakes. The maze turned baffling, branching off in odd directions. Too many wrong turns, wrong directions, and they could be lost, seriously lost, in danger, and so they surveyed the maze, learned it like a language, mapped it out like land. They taught themselves its contours, twists, and tricks, until it could not trick them anymore. Gradually, the maze looked different to them. It was theirs, by grace, by gift.

They claimed it as holy ground.

+++

ENCOUNTERING THE MYSTERY

Certain stories stay with us. They take up lodgings in the soul and remain as quiet guests, unobtrusive, waiting to be summoned. For me, one such story is about the Christian catacombs; it lodged, it stayed, on call—then turned into a shocker: the story broke out, pushed forward, and demanded to be heard again. Startled, I listened. I listened again. This time, I heard more than ever before. The story had a different, deeper meaning for me. In the end, the rediscovered story helped to transform my image of depression.

21

I had often wished to *see* depression; if I saw it, perhaps I could make more sense of it. Now, conjured by the story, its image appeared: a great maze, like the catacombs, below the ground, a vast network of passageways in seamless darkness.

This maze is a striking symbol. It images depression for us, so that we can *see* what we are facing. Seeing gives us more power. The maze has an outline. It has a shape. Many studies show that our minds relate first and foremost to images. Through this one, the maze, we can view some crucial aspects of depression:

There, we see its darkened inner world, its narrow passages closing around us, leading down, down into hopelessness, where we wander, knowing we are lost. Here, projected on the dark, are remnants of the past: every mistake, every regret, every failure rises here. Down another level, the dampness clings, chilling as self-hatred.

We are alone here, radically alone, stumbling onward, not knowing why. Nothing seems to matter now. Clearly, God has abandoned us; God is far away. On a stretch of rough ground we falter, fall, and cannot rise. We crouch, immobilized, hopeless. The maze, it seems, has won ... but not forever.

We will survey this place, map it, know it, as the early Christians did within the catacombs. Like them, we will find our way here. We will find the signs and patterns that we need, and we will find that we are not alone, exiles, stumbling in the dark.

Maze as Spiritual Mirror

The early Christians saw the catacombs with daring vision. They knew this was a place of death, decay, and mourning, but they could also see it as a place of encounter with God. Famed religious historian Mircea

Eliade asserts that wherever humanity encounters the holy, that is holy ground. "The place is never `chosen'.... In other words, the sacred place in some way or another reveals itself."

But—this place? This ground? This place was not decent. This was not a place fit for the living. Within its walls were decomposing corpses. For the holy, for the sacred, for worship, it seems clearly out of bounds.

We can feel the same way about depression. As a state of mind, it seems shameful. No matter what we have learned, we may still see depression as *a spiritual failure.* Perhaps, if our faith were stronger, we would not succumb to depression. If we prayed more often, if we were more spiritual, depression might not find a way to get at us.

Depression now seems like a form of *temptation,* one we are too weak to resist. Until we get this "under control," we may feel spiritually degraded and distanced. It helps to know that depression is not a matter of will or morality or character. If our brain chemistry is off-balance, our problem is biochemical, not a spiritual lapse. Still, this raises a significant point about spirituality and depression.

When the early Christians worshiped in the catacombs, they did not feel disgraced, however others perceived them. Their Sunday eucharists were usually held in house-churches, but these Christians came to the catacombs on feast days. In this perpetual darkness, they came to honor their heroes of faith. Here, they felt a special sense of Christ's passion. His presence was with them all here, the dead and the living. They felt that presence and they came, unashamed.

Jesus had come to people and places declared off-limits, ritually "unclean," "low class," out of bounds. However, Jesus drew no such distinctions, nor did his followers. The good news was clear to them. *In the catacombs and in depression, in all states of mind, we are never off-limits to God.* In the beatitudes, God exalts what the world stigmatizes. As we begin to absorb this, we may feel less reluctant to open our depressive feelings to God. We may feel relief, release, and then, perhaps, a delayed reaction—shock and even anger. We realize that we face an illness, a real illness that may be chronic, recurring, requiring treatment. Is this really good news? New questions arise.

Why me?
Why depression?
Why does it happen?

Taking the Measure of the Maze
Hardly anyone escapes depression.

It affects most of us, sometime in life, firsthand or though someone we know. "Since 1915, the risk of depression has increased worldwide, nearly doubling for each successive generation," write William and Lucy Hulme, in *Wrestling With Depression.* Depression, however, has appeared in every era, noted in the Old Testament and in ancient Greece, noted by Hippocrates, the father of Western medicine. Depression seems interwoven with the human condition. People have been trudging through its maze for a very long time, no matter who they are or what they do—people of all races, ages, classes, cultures, talents, abilities, and genders (although depression is more prevalent in women). Depression, that great leveler, has never been alien to us. Perhaps, in part, because it has often been concealed or closeted, we have seldom understood it.

Instead, depression seems to mystify us. Once it was attributed to "Black Bile," which translates to "melancholia." Also called "the vapors" and "the lying down disease," depression has been mistaken for madness, idiocy, and demonic possession. However it was labeled, it was a stigma to hide and lock away.

In our age of medical sophistication, we are less inclined to view depression as demonic possession (although some religious denominations hold this belief). But in many workplaces, professions, and social circles depression is still unacceptable and detrimental to one's reputation and security. The illness is often miscast in terrifying roles—the madwoman locked in the attic, the brooding loner with the gun. Stereotypes like these hang back now, but they do hang on. We may have to admit that we know less about depression than we suppose.

Mood or Maze?

In the twentieth century, we confused depression with "the blues," "the blahs," "funks," and "lows." There is a widespread belief that people with depression, even in its major form, simply need to pull themselves together, snap out of it, lighten up, get a grip, get a life. My personal favorite is, "Come on—it's all in your mind."

Well, yes, but it isn't something we can simply "snap" out of or will away. Its debilitating effects are real, as noted by acclaimed author William Styron, writing about his suicidal depression in *Darkness Visible*. It can actually be dangerous to brush off depression as a mere funk. Unattended, depression almost always worsens, and if it is serious, self-destructive thoughts can easily arise. How, then, do we distinguish depression from normal sadness, from feeling "low" or "down"?

Normal sadness and normal "lows" are relatively brief responses, far less pervasive, and potentially less self-destructive than a depression. Common sadness does not interfere with your ability to feel pleasure or motivation or a lift from an outside source. In depression, there is *anhedonia,* a clinical term for lack of pleasure in anything, even from usual sources like music or lunch with a friend. One's sense of motivation also slips away in depression. "What's the point?" is a common feeling. Outside events provide no relief. Brief "low" moods come and go as normal parts of life. If these moods had an image, they might be revolving doors. Depression has no doors. It has walls. It has its own power. It still seems somewhat mysterious, almost mythic, like a visit from the Greek Furies, those great legendary tormenters from ancient Greek drama.

The Maze Revealed
Take away the myths and mystery.
What really lies beneath them?
Solid fact: Depression is actually *a medical illness.* Like other illnesses, it has different forms: acute, chronic, recurring. It has degrees, from mild to moderate to major. It may be "reactive," set off by an event. It may be "clinical," a chemical depression coming on for no apparent reason. There is "bipolar" or "manic depression," characterized by mood swings between highs and lows, or the constant low condition (unipolar) we address here. In depression's most serious forms, with suicidal features, hospitalization may be required.
Who gets the visits from the Furies? How many of us suffer from what Winston Churchill called his depression, the "Black Dog"?
Depression affects a great many of us: one in five Americans, or about twenty million people, according to the Surgeon General, who admits to "conservative" estimates. Depressive illness is a top cause of disability, worldwide, and *the* top cause of suicide in this country.
The good news: depression responds well to treatment (eighty percent success), although only fifty percent of

depressed people seek treatment. Depression is now widely accepted as *a legitimate illness* by the health care community and the Surgeon General. Slowly, several other sectors, at different rates, are accepting depression as an illness as well. This slow but crucial change affects the way we see depression and the way depressed people, including me, see themselves.

What a relief, at last, to learn that depression is not moral weakness, or the outward sign of our inner "wrong-think," in Joan Didion's apt term. It is liberating to know what depression is—and what it is not: not weakness, not punishment, not insanity, in any form.

Nor is it "a figment of the imagination." I was told this often, as an adolescent, when clinical depression often begins. As one of those artistic types, I was, of course, suspect. We were "sensitive." We spent too much time alone, scribbling stories and having figments. Never mind; I didn't have them—I only *imagined* them. So I was told. Shyness, sensitivity, and "feeling down," in my family, were seen as social liabilities or "problem child" behavior, and so, such feelings were briskly discounted and swiftly dismissed, as if they might leave a stain. This presented me with a confusing problem:

These feelings I didn't have were real.

I was not supposed to have them, but I did; I could only conclude that this was my fault. "When we are gripped by depression, we may feel the added burden and guilt of not being able to pull out of it," write pastoral counselors Rachel Callahan and Rea McDonnell. It takes some time to absorb the new facts: Depression is an illness—not misbehavior, not something that we're doing wrong.

Alma Powell, wife of General Colin Powell, spoke movingly about her depressive illness, controlled by medication: "Now I can say, 'This is not my fault,' " she stated publicly, showing great courage. She spoke for many people and for us all, spoke liberating words.

Such insights have an impact on the whole person. The spiritual dimension of our lives is touched, as noted, along with body and mind. Somehow, we may harbor a fear that depression is a fall from grace, an outward sign of spiritual failure or divine punishment. We may also feel deeply estranged from God; we may interpret depression as penance.

Suppressing or denying our anger, we may feel estranged from God for a long time. To address this, we need to look at everything again from a new angle.

THE MAZE, DEMYSTIFIED

For centuries, there were no accurate answers. In this century, psychology has brought insight and, since the 1950s, there have been breakthroughs in medication to treat depression by balancing brain chemistry; further breakthroughs in this field have come in the last twenty years. In addition, there have been remarkable advances in what we know about the brain itself, its structure and function. There have also been tremendous discoveries about the role of genetic "programming" in relation to illness. All these factors bring us to a new understanding of depression's "mystery."

Now there is a general medical consensus on the cause of most depressions: imbalanced brain chemistry, much of it determined by heredity, genetic coding, or "familial tendencies."

Dr. Alen J. Salerian, director of the Psychiatric Institute of Washington, D.C., estimates that eighty percent of all depressions are rooted in two factors: biochemistry and heredity. These views are corroborated by Dr. David Pickar, of the National Institutes of Mental Health. The

Surgeon General's recent report also cites brain chemistry and familial predisposition as the major causes for depression, although his percentages are somewhat more conservative.

Are we doomed, then, by our own brains? Not at all. A range of medications can balance the brain's biochemistry, medications proven in demanding clinical trials. It is important to note here and elsewhere that there is often resistance to taking these medications. We need to be clear that antidepressants do not cause highs or any results associated with "recreational drugs." Antidepressants and augmenting medication do not steal the soul or turn you into someone else. The medications actually return you to yourself, normalizing your brain chemistry. The right medications can manage depression much as insulin manages diabetes. A combination of psychotherapy and medication has just been endorsed by a major study conducted by the *New England Journal of Medicine.*

The outlook for depression is more hopeful than ever before. Even with genetic predispositions, we do not necessarily replicate the depressions of the previous generation. For example, my father's depression was far more severe and complex than mine. His father's illness was different yet again. If you have a family history of depression, you do not necessarily replicate someone else's profile of depression, and other factors can mitigate it.

In fact, you may be predisposed to depression, but it may never become manifest. If it does, it may be mild. It may not be chronic or cyclical. You may have a single depressive episode and never have another. Even if your depression is chronic and severe, you have the best treatment options yet available.

It is also true that you have a far greater chance of depression if one of your "first degree" relatives had depression. Intense prolonged stress and trauma can set off depression. An acute "reactive" depression (to an event) can become chronic. If you have more than one recurrence of depression, you are likely to have more. Now, however, there are many resources to meet these challenges.

As I look back just twenty years, I see how far we have come. I think of this as I look back at my glamorous, beautiful aunt, whom I watched with girlish admiration. Clearly, she was perfect and I hoped that someday I could be just like her.

Trauma and Tragedy

She had a way of moving: fluid, subtle, elegant. I studied the twine of her hair, the striking simple clothes, the way she smoked a cigarette and smiled into my eyes. Her red lipstick left half-moons on her glass; she drank Scotch straight, like a man. She had a "big" career in fashion; she had a quiet spiritual life. At Mass, she knelt within her own stillness, like a crystal shell. I never thought it could shatter.

Suddenly, the adults were whispering. My aunt's mother, in anger, disowned her, then died. My aunt plunged into a suicidal depression. From a psychiatric hospital, she sent me small gifts she had made: wires strung with beads, shaped into circles and stars. Then the gifts stopped. There were to be no more. My aunt never recovered, was in an out of hospitals for most of her life.

I still think of her. It is not her face I see now I see a half-moon on a Scotch glass; I see a perfect circle of turquoise beads.

This tragedy is a worst-case scenario, not the norm. This is also a case of depression that developed complications. Now I see how trauma set off my aunt's dormant illness. I learned that there had been warning signs, all overlooked, and a family history of her illness, unmentioned.

Today, such a case would have had different treatment, and most likely different results. Still, this is a cautionary tale. It warns us all not to wait for a crisis, but to learn depression's symptoms. It urges us to find *some way* of talking about depression *somehow*. *I* guess we always think such things just won't happen. Not in our family. Not to us. Of course, they do—to us and those around us, to people who appear to "have it all."

Moreover, as I learned, such crises happen to *prayerful* people, people of committed faith. Of course, we know that, but sometimes we are surprised when such people are subject to depression. Doesn't their faith ward it off? How can a priest or a nun be depressed? I once heard a doctor tell a new seminarian that there would be no more need of a mild sleeping medication; the vocation would take care of any troubles now.

"Some people still think religion is magic," a Carmelite prioress remarked to me. "God also works through *medicine.*" She knew. She had experienced severe clinical depression; she was predisposed to it by heredity, but the illness did not surface until her early forties. Several years into her life as a contemplative nun, she was severely debilitated.

However, she sought treatment for spirit, mind, and body from a top psychiatrist—who happened to be another Carmelite. Medication was the decisive factor in recovery, which of course included spiritual attention. When it was time to elect a new prioress, there was no doubt in her community that she would be a great and gifted prioress, and so she was. Among many others whose lives she touched, I will never forget her. I remember visiting with her in a simple room, surrounded by stillness. "I like quiet miracles," she said that day. To appreciate God's quiet miracles, and to understand depression's mechanics, we must look into another maze. A marvel: the brain.

Messengers Within the Maze

Today, we know more about the brain than ever before. We know, of course, that the brain has different sectors, with different primary functions. The middle brain, for example, has a lot to do with short-term memory. Our special interest lies with the cerebral cortex and its complex network of minuscule "circuits."

The smallest of these "circuits" are called neurons. As in a maze, they crisscross and intersect and link, although there are microscopic gaps, called synapses, between them. Chemicals are always moving through the brain's circuitry, carrying innumerable messages, each message coded electrochemically.

Neurotransmitters are the chemicals that move through the neurons and, importantly, cross those tiny synaptic gaps. Specific neurotransmitters carry messages pertaining to mood and depression. Three major neuro-transmitters are usually cited in relation to depression: dopamine, serotonin, and norepinephrine.

Getting the Right Messages

Simply put, the serotonin levels fall and *if the levels of these neurotransmitters are too low or imbalanced, we are likely to experience depression.* Hormones also play an important part, including estrogen, testosterone, and thyroxin. A sluggish thyroid can be another factor in depression, as well as levels of light and blood sugar.

Neurotransmitters are related to emotions. Low serotonin levels can cause many conditions, such as obsessive compulsive disorders. Among its many func-tions, low levels of dopamine can affect our ability to feel motivation and pleasure. A drop in norepinephrine can cause us to feel inertia, drowsiness, and general lethargy, which can be accentuated by a sluggish thyroid. Clearly, biochemistry plays a large role in depression. A lot goes on "behind the scenes," a lot more that is beyond this book's purview. We have a basic background now to use as we move from the biochemical perspective to others.

A Maze of Mixed Emotions

The maze winds on, leading to other theories of depression's causes. As we turn to psychological and cognitive approaches, we find certain constants that transcend gender, race, culture—constants of the human condition.

Loss and abuse are almost always seen as factors in depression. Significant childhood losses can have lasting depressive effects, especially the loss of a parent. William Styron relates the early loss of his mother to his suicidal depression. Unresolved conflicts and traumas (especially abuse) can also contribute to depression, especially if the pain remains unexpressed.

Most experts emphasize the role of repressed emotions in depression. A well-respected theory focuses on repressed anger. It is thought that repressed anger can turn inward and become inverted, manifesting as depression. Repressed grief and trauma, especially rape, abuse, and group humiliation, may generate depression long after the causative event.

Trauma and Depression

Posttraumatic stress disorder may contribute to depression in children and adults. Some of its features are nightmares and flashbacks, as well as affective disorders. Soldiers have experienced this syndrome after combat, long before the condition had this name. Other more subtle kinds of trauma can also cause PTSD, such as deliberate humiliation by a group of peers, combined with rejection and/or job loss. For depression, then, repressed emotions and intense stress seem to be important factors. In the brain's complex maze, we have seen how such factors travel like messages. If depression were not so debilitating, it might fascinate us. Now, however, we move on to something simpler for us; something bright and external.

'Tis the Season to Be Sad

Available, ordinary, simple, sunlight's absence can cause "seasonal depression," or seasonal affective disorder. Some people are very sensitive to light and feel depressed if they do not get enough full-spectrum light. Twenty minutes of outdoor light is good for anyone with depressive tendencies. Light therapy (with a light box) gets good reviews from those with mild depression. For moderate and severe depression, more aggressive treatment is needed.

It is well known that people in sunny climates have lower incidences of depression, while societies with shorter summers and less light are statistically higher in depression. If you have mild depression or SAD, you might try full-spectrum light bulbs or a light box.

What Do You Think?

Cognitive behavioral theory (CBT) asserts that our thoughts' content and patterns cause depression. David Burns, in *The New Mood Therapy,* cites many forms of irrational negative "self-talk" and negative thinking. CBT works to change such patterns, such as "catastrophizing" fears or situations, "overgeneralizing" and looking at life through a "negative filter" or exaggerating a possible negative outcome to an event and other kinds of negative thinking. CBT works with symptoms, not underlying causes.

THE GOOD SHEPHERD

Among causes and neurons and symptoms, where, in all of this, is God? When I ask myself that, I see one persistent image: the figure of a man who carries a lamb on his shoulders: Jesus, the Good Shepherd, painted on the catacombs' walls.

The figure keeps appearing, down a tunnel, in another space, at another turn. You go a little further and there again, he watches from another wall. A gentle figure and a strong one, smiling, carrying the lost sheep he has gone to find; carrying it as a father carries a small child. On many walls, in many sections, he is there.

In depression, in treatment, God is everywhere—but I don't always notice. I don't always recognize that smile, that face. I may be too discouraged to look up. I may be too anxious, too intent on my struggle to be aware of God's presence all around me.

But I recognize that sheep.

I know that sheep. I am sensitized now to the look of certain lost ones; those lost in depression. In the doctor's waiting room alone, I have seen many different faces of depression. I would recognize its features in another setting; I have seen it often enough in the mirror.

Sometimes, my doctor must shift one of my medications. Occasionally, I have a brief relapse and I fear that I will slide all the way back. At such times, I have learned to focus on the image of the smiling shepherd. Not only does he bring back the lost. He carries them. He holds them. He smiles. He reappears. He reappears again. I see no miraculous images. No dramatic cures. A man finding and holding the lost—that is all I see. Somehow, that is everything.

Now we turn from inner images to outward signs of depression. We will look at symptoms that send signals we can miss. What is your image of God as you *approach* this section? What is it *after* this section, if you find you have several of depression's symptoms?

Signposts in the Maze
Signs are easy to miss. It just happens.
Messages are easy to miss; it happens.
It also happens that things shift so subtly, so smoothly, we don't notice right away. When did we start feeling empty and unsteady, what was the first sign? We seem about to skid, to fall.
We walk through the days as if on ice. *Everything okay?* people ask. *Of course,* we *say, Fine, fine,* but we have lost the walk, the look, the stride, the illusion of control. Life seems to slope now, down and down, but, oh sure, we're fine.

Reading the Signs
Us? Depressed? No way.
Our first reaction is denial. Why do we ignore the signs?
Perhaps depression does not fit with our self-image. We tell ourselves that we're too tough. Too sensible, too smart. Too blessed with the good life; too whatever. Perhaps we feel ashamed to name what we feel, or we may fear that others will not accept us if we are less than upbeat, and so we dissemble. Depressed? Who, *me?*
If we are open or just lucky, we note signs too insistent to ignore. There is a basic core of symptoms that indicate depression, whatever its degree or kind. No list can capture a complex condition. Even so, experts find this list is a good indicator. Depression is likely if you have most of these symptoms:

- Feelings of pervasive, persistent sadness.
- Constant lack pleasure, enjoyment, motivation.
- Changes in sleeping and eating patterns.
- Difficulty concentrating and thinking clearly.
- Social withdrawal and a tendency to isolate.
- Feeling persistently worthless, hopeless, helpless.
- Constant lethargy, lack of energy, fatigue.
- Lowered libido.
- Thoughts of death and suicide.

Sometimes, there are accompanying symptoms, such as anxiety.

Following the Signs. . . or Not

A respected therapist, Martha Manning, wrote about her shock at her own "score" on a similar list. *All* the symptoms applied to her. At first she was unable to believe it. She was the healer; others brought such symptoms to her. She checked out her findings. Her diagnosis was clear. She had major depression.

The therapist, the healer, the authority, became the patient. Now she had to deal with her own personal depression. Because she pressed on early, past denial, she recovered from her depression after ECT (electro-convulsive shock therapy). Her book *Undercurrents is* a brave and honest account of her experience. She is a therapist again, helping others with more insight than ever before.

Taking a Bypass

Martha Manning's story contrasts sharply with the story of a surgeon, brilliant, gifted, and expert at diagnosis. Other surgeons often came to his home for advice on their own cases. One evening, a visitor appeared: the surgeon's friend, a psychiatrist. The two men talked, engrossed, unaware of anyone nearby. One word was repeated by the psychiatrist. Voices rose. The surgeon ordered his friend out of his house.

The surgeon fumed: an insult. An affront. A lie, a lie. He would blot it out. This evening never happened. The surgeon kept his secret: serious depression, his friend had said, trying to help. This depression was a great darkness that usually came only in private. He died, too young, within this darkness. Only later, it was named.

The surgeon was my father. I was in the doorway when I heard that word spoken and repeated by his concerned friend: *depression*. A self-made man, my father believed in will and self-control. No force would control him. He was the healer, not the patient. He may have feared for his practice, despite his friend's oath of confidentiality. In any case, my father's life was tragically affected by this illness he denied. Unlike Dr. Manning, he could not be who he was and have depression.

This is another cautionary tale. It saddens me more than ever, but it warns us to heed symptoms. Ironically, my father felt strongly about this in his own practice, urging patients to catch illness early. Healer that he was, he would urge you to heed the signs, then take the road he missed.

As you think about the list of symptoms, I hope you can see them as *positive* signs, pointing to healing, not to weakness. After shock and disbelief, we have a choice. My father's choice was very costly. Yours need not be so.

Dealing With Darkness

By now, you know more—but may feel worse. Mazes, even the most beautiful, can make you feel lost, frustrated, and discouraged, whether they twine through gardens, cathedrals, or the catacombs.

When I fully faced my symptoms and depression, I was overwhelmed. This was an enormous maze, and I did not know the pattern. This was a serious illness, not a passing phase, and I knew what happened when it was ignored within my family. I had to keep on struggling, but I felt too dispirited to try.

That was when I started thinking of the Christians in the catacombs. In modern parlance, I wondered how they "treated" depression. They faced life's ordinary sorrows in addition to extraordinary persecutions. Heroic as they were, they were also human. As devout believers, they would have turned to prayer.

Even so, there would have been pain. In their humanity, with loss after loss, missing faces, silenced voices—how did they find consolation?

Stories in the Dark

They did what people have always done.

They told stories in the dark.

If someone gave his or her life for the faith, there would be a kind of wake at the martyr's tomb. The community would gather there, within the catacombs. There might be eucharist and a meal. Lights were kindled, stories told: the story of this hero and his death, and then, the stories of this man and his life, this comrade, this neighbor, perhaps the cobbler or the vintner up the street.

His brothers and sisters in faith tell how bravely he died. Then they talk of how he cobbled shoes, fed cats, and how he roared with laughter, hated rain, stopped a thief, or spilled the soup ... and through the story's power, something happens. Glory merges with the ordinary. Life merges with death. A lost friend seems to draw near once again.

"We tell stories in order to live," writes Joan Didion, the noted author. I believe we also tell stories in order to *live with the dark. I* have learned this as a writer and a teacher of writing, but sometimes, I forget. The stories of the catacombs reminded me once more.

If we tell our story, the story of this struggle with depression, we may find much needed catharsis and consolation. If we tell this story in a private notebook, or to a friend, we bring the story out into the light, where it loses its sense of mystery and power. We can find inspiration from the early Christians. They set words to pain, as if to music. They made stories of the dark. So can we.

The Courage to Seek Treatment

As you consider treatment, you may want to back out. You may hate doctors. You hate sharing personal stuff with strangers. You hate medication; you never take more than aspirin. You don't have time for therapy. What if people you know find out? Maybe this treatment thing isn't for you.

I dreaded sounding like "a case." I feared a diagnosis that would make me a cross between Mrs. Rochester and Mrs. Danvers (the mad women from *Jane Eyre* and *Rebecca),* but I was in enough distress to override my resistance. I hope you can overcome yours. You have many options, wide in range, well-tested, and more available than ever before. If one way is wrong for you, there are others.

Maze and Grace

That is not all there is to it. Our spiritual selves also need healing. Depression wounds the whole person. The spiritual dimension is often neglected, but in the maze, in the darkness, there are gifts of the spirit to discover. Once more, I find insight from the catacombs.

In this place of endings, early Christians called forth new creations. On the surface of the grave-lined walls, they created timeless art. Here, amid the tombs, Christian artists painted stories of Good News. Good news—here? The very walls shout *Yes.*

Crouching in the chilly darkness, men lit torches and mixed pigments. In the rippling light, scenes emerged from the dim walls. "Behold, I do a new thing, now it comes forth," *the prophet speaks for God.*

In the catacombs, it is the paintings that speak. They are a kind of visual prophecy, pointing ahead to the spiritual world, to the resurrection, to new life, to holy souls who raise their arms in joyous prayer. These paintings and frescoes served to express and inspire faith. One series is a condensed gospel in images. The good news, told in pictures, was important to the many early Christians who could not read.

Once more, these tableaus remind us of God's limitless presence. They also remind us of God's creative action, always drawing life from barrenness and devastation. In the depths of these dark labyrinths, only life and hope are imaged: fishermen and baptism and the Good Shepherd. Here again, in these places of death, we find ourselves caught up in life's encounter with the holy, as artists and worshipers were two thousand years ago.

Amid these galleries of graves, centered in this blackness, this artwork glows—a stunning symbol of spirituality in the midst of depression. This is how depressive illness can look: not dense, not totally despairing, but encircling rich spiritual life—life that grows in the dark.

The early Christian artists turned their faith and their struggle into art. Here, again, we see God's unending reach into our darkness, be it persecution or depression. To remind us, these paintings appear before us, a great many paintings, in this honeycomb of tombs, spread across the bone-packed walls, carved deep within the earth.

This is a quiet miracle on these walls, in these painted images of life. Here are these new creations wrought in darkness: wrested just as we can be, forever.

■

THREE

Unlocking the Door:
Vigils and Depression

Gray men in a gray room behind a locked door.
Here they are, hiding out: the disciples of Jesus. Here
they have been since Gethsemane. No lamps are lit. No
one moves. Light from small windows, set high, settles
like ash over them all.

Peter glances at his comrades. The seem to have a
aged and grown frail. Their faces have the pinched,
cautious look of old beggars. Sounds below in the street
make them flinch. Is Jerusalem still dangerous? Was it
ever dangerous—for them? No one goes to find out.
Instead, they sit silent. Like Lot's wife, they have looked
back. Now they cannot look forward, nor can they look at
one another.

The women have brought food and news, as did John,
and the terrible story has been told. The disciples have
pictured it all, every scene. In every scene, they are
missing. The future is missing. Sickening gaps have

appeared. Jesus, gone? Their plans, their part in a great endeavor—all are gone. There are moments, even hours when they cannot believe it, and so they sit in silence and try not to think of the past or the future. There is only the present; only this room.

Now, it is Sunday, and nothing has changed. No one believes Mary Magdalene's sad little tale: she was overwrought, overtired. Too much strain, little sleep—no wonder she mistook the gardener for Jesus. The tomb's owner must have moved the body, made new plans, that was all. She was sent off to rest. The door was locked, the silence continues.

This is their first morning, Peter realizes, without prayer. Their Sabbath was a poor one; they had not even lit the lamps. From boyhood, Peter recalls widening circles of Sabbath lamplight and later, in the Temple, those great lamps burning as men kept vigil, . . . *in your light we see light* . . . may my *prayer rise as incense*. . . .

Now, abruptly, he rises and lights the room's largest lamp. He starts a prayer, his voice low, then stronger, fuller—not just his voice now, their voices lift. A psalm is offered, then a prayer; the men are coming together again. *"Be still before the Lord and wait patiently for him. . . ."* For what do they wait? For Jesus to rise? They doubt; they don't know. But now they seek God's word and their voices fade into silent prayer: they are waiting on God, as in a vigil.

Peter looks at the others again.

Light touches their faces.

The gray room is no longer gray.

DANCING IN THE DARK

As child, girl, and young woman, I lit countless candles in a great cathedral. There, in the nave, it was always twilight and prayer always echoed, and there was always the smell of floor wax, flowers, and incense. Everywhere there were banks of jigging, joyous vigil candles.

Why did I light them? I could not explain. Maybe, as a child, I thought of the candles as prayers I could see; prayers that lasted into the night and into the darkness I feared. Often, after bedtime, I lay awake, gazing out at the huge night sky, a great black ocean that might draw me in and drown me in its depths. Whenever this fear came, I would close my eyes and picture all the vigil candles I had ever lit, maybe a million; maybe a billion. I would see them in row upon row upon row, great walls of fire against the strong pull of the dark.

In my mind I still see the cathedral, though I have not lived in its vicinity for years. I see it at random, in dreams, in peace. At times, I summon the cathedral when I am struggling, when I need a haven, my spired island of childhood. It has always been there for me, except for that one time I tried to summon it as usual, but the usual response failed.

A Season of Sorrow

A season of sorrow came for me, a few years ago, a strange stubborn season, one that settled in and stayed. I summoned the cathedral to mind—the blue air, the scent, the soaring space. No image came. I summoned the candles, once so strong against the dark, but again, nothing. This had never happened, and I had never needed the cathedral more. I was struggling with clinical depression, a darkness far stronger than all the night skies of my childhood.

I began to light my own candles, morning and evening, near a small icon by my desk. Sometimes the icon's golden background shimmered in the candle's light. Somehow this made me feel a little better. Once again, light was prayer, prayer was light.

My own prayers, short and simple, relied heavily on one word: *"Help."* I found a box of well-loved spiritual books. I read. I slept. Lunch was a major event. The days stretched ahead like an empty highway. In a state of quiet desolation, I could not work. Immobilized by the depression, I sat on the couch in the study for much of the day and watched the candle. I had few thoughts, fewer insights. But there, I did come to one realization: *Depression is always a locked room.*

Meanwhile, in my own locked room, it was a time of waiting, a time of watching. My depression wore on; I could not concentrate on much for long, though I could read and write for brief intervals. I watched the tracery of bare tree branches, and I watched the depression's course. In this minor action, alone, I felt somewhat useful, somewhat closer to my former life as a functioning, responsible adult.

For my doctor, I began a daily log, a kind of "fever chart" for the depression's course, its daily cycles, ups and downs, or rather lows and "higher lows," and the effects of medication. I started to look forward to these entries; I was actually "doing something" when I wrote entries.

I made several entries each day. This small act, every few hours, seemed to order time, segmenting the long days. I started to add other entries: a thought or two— such as they were—a line of prayer, a note about some reading. Moving to the desk, I wrote haltingly in the candle's half-circle of light.

The depression remained, I knew, but something new was happening.

Reaching for Spiritual Resources

Time was taking on a certain pattern. The log, the prayers, the regular readings and reflections seemed to give the day a rhythm. The rhythm held, even through a setback. No doubt, I prolonged it with a careless act: a glance in the mirror. I looked like a cover girl for the collected works of Edgar Allan Poe. I fled.

Sitting on the couch, I closed my eyes and summoned the cathedral's image once again. Nothing. I opened my log to warn myself away from mirrors. I didn't need them. I had easily gone a week without a mirror when I was at St. Sophia's, a breathtaking convent, set in brilliant gardens, near the sea.

The prioress, a friend, invited me to follow the convent's rhythm: prayer and work, reading and reflection. There were seven times or "hours" of daily communal prayer. The first started the day's rhythm while it was still dark out, long before dawn. Tactfully, the prioress added, I might choose to ramble on my own.

I chose to follow their rhythm, and by accident or Providence, I entered a time so luminous, it could only happen once. The week was pure gift; a graced time, unlike any other. I can never manage to fit it into words. At week's end, I felt bereft. My visit, I knew, was an exception. The convent was far from home; I would not be back. At the door, the prioress took my hand. "There are other places." She looked pensive. "Find this," she pointed behind her, "out there."

"Find *this? No way,*" I thought. She saw. "You can, you know." Her blue eyes glinted. Her tone said, *I dare you.*

Groping for Grace

Now, thinking back on it all, I actually laughed.

I had summoned *the wrong sanctuary.*

47

I had tried to summon the cathedral. Instead, I got the convent. Some spiritual circuits had crossed—and perhaps that was an answer to prayer: the right sanctuary at the right time, after all.

There are other places.

I recalled the convent's gardens, the old stone cloister, the sea. There are other places. I could see the prioress, tall, straight, weathered, framed by the arched doorway. *Find this out there.* Her face serene; her voice sassy.

You can, you know.

I had never tried. Now, through the gift of grace and memory, my locked room was giving way to new yet familiar terrain.

What I had done, in desperation, was to grope for what had restored me before. My new pattern, I saw now, was not so new, nor was it mine. The pattern was clearly related to that week of grace, which in turn was based on time-honored monastic practice. On some level, I still drew on that week for inspiration, and somehow, it had led me into a particular pattern. Finally, I realized its name: a vigil.

That's what it was—a *vigil of depression.*

Throughout that long depression and several medication try-outs, the vigil form supported me. It lasted. It flexed to my pace. It did not rush me or bog me down. Little by little, it helped me to emerge from my "locked room." It seemed to anchor me, and in all these ways, it was consistent. The vigil form was consistently helpful, even a saving grace, but I knew little about the practice. I could recognize a vigil but could not explain one.

What did it actually mean "to keep vigil"? Why, when, and how were they kept? Why is this tradition so honored?

VIGILS: TIMELESS VENTURES OF SPIRIT

Our word "vigil" derives from the Latin *vigilia*. It means "watchful" or "awake," especially in the sense of spiritual alertness. *Vigilia* can also signify "watching over or with someone" who may be off-guard, ill, or asleep. Finally, there is a general secular meaning to vigil: staying awake at a time when it is usual to sleep or retire. That meaning has changed over time, and vigils are no longer restricted to the night. Keeping vigil is an age-old tradition, with a rich history.

Spiritual vigils pre-date Christianity. In northern Europe, people would kindle huge bonfires on the hilltops in early spring. This was a sign of hope and also a plea to the deity, Woden, to bring the earth back to life. St. Patrick "baptized" the custom into Celtic Christianity by kindling Easter's new light as a hilltop bonfire at Tara, seat of pagan kings.

In the Judeo-Christian tradition, vigils have a long history. As noted, they were kept in the Temple, where carved cherubim flanked the Ark to symbolize God's protection in the darkness, which contrasts with "the glory of the Lord's presence." Certain psalms were used in vigils, such as Psalm 17: "Keep me as the apple of your eye; hide me under the shadow of your wings. . . ." Silent prayer also played an important role. The scriptures often speak of waiting on God in silence.

In early Christian worship keeping watch for God had an added connotation. The return of Christ was seen as immanent, and the church wanted to be alert to the final coming. As the centuries passed, that concern has receded. For us, what matters is the presence of Jesus with us now—and still to come in fullness. We live in the paradox of Christ who is with us, "already but not yet."

In the meantime, the early church celebrated the resurrection with joy. The Vigil of Easter, "the mother of all vigils," in St. Augustine's words, was the apex of the church year and a time for baptisms. The feast day of a martyr was another occasion for a vigil in the catacombs. When persecution ended with Constantine's edict in 312 A.D., vigils became more public. Throughout the night, the community prepared for the feast with prayers, scripture readings, silent reflection, a sermon, and eucharist. After a morning break, the feast itself was celebrated in the afternoon. Monastic practice helped to shape church vigils, seventeen of which were observed each year through the Middle Ages and into the last century. The tradition of keeping vigil before the eucharist was also popular and continues today in many parishes.

The Easter Vigil: Darkness and Light

For centuries, in many parts of Europe, everything went dark on Good Friday. At three o'clock on that day, the candle was put out under the family crucifix and all other lights in the home were extinguished, including all hearth fires. The lights in the church were likewise put out. No light was kindled until the new fire of the Easter Vigil. This, the most ancient and honored liturgical vigil, was celebrated through the entire night, beginning after dark on Holy Saturday until Easter morning.

The Good Friday liturgy was often conducted by memory, at night, in the dark church, as it was for part of Maundy Thursday. Then at the Easter Vigil, imagine the impact of the new fire and the Paschal candle in that darkness. In many parts of Europe, it was customary to bring a brand of the new Easter fire back to the home. This holy fire would first rekindle the hearth and from the hearth all other lights in the house.

This movement from darkness to light mirrors our own experience of depression and our hopes for recovery. We are in the dark and yet, even there, on some level of our being, we hope—even if we do not name it, even if we do not admit it, we still hope, like the disciples in their dim locked room.

The Power of Personal Vigils

Less visible, but no less rich, personal vigils have always been kept. The quieter sister to communal practice, the vigil form is well suited to individual spirituality. The personal vigil is a hidden gem, flexible but not facile, sacred but not somber. To me, this discipline, helpful for anyone, is particularly helpful for people in depression. Personal vigils can also help people dealing with other long-term illness.

An Offering of Time and Presence

The vigil format is flexible; simple rituals are often added. Daily vigils are usually kept morning and evening over the course of a few days, perhaps a week, perhaps longer. A single vigil is sometimes kept for several consecutive hours, marking a holy day or as a eucharistic devotion.

A vigil is an offering of your time and presence. This time is dedicated to be specially aware of God, in varied ways. Vigils can be held on any day, at any time—not restricted to nights. The amount of time you devote depends on you. Simply do what you can, what works best for you. Monks traditionally kept vigil throughout the night, a time of quiet, conducive to reflection and meditation. You might make a special night vigil if you like, but the time of day is far less important than the vigil itself.

Such a rich part of our tradition, it's no wonder, then, that vigils help us bear with depression. I kept daily vigils through depression, in short intervals, morning, noon, and evening; morning and evening is more common. For me, the vigils structured the day and engaged me as I selected readings and prayers. I also liked the continuity of the form, a steady rhythm, throughout the fluctuations of illness. A vigil can be kept in many ways, loosely or detailed, and can go on as long as needed, like a strong thread running through the days and nights.

To see that thread more clearly, you may want to keep a journal. Your observations can be helpful to your doctor. Writing out your thoughts can be very helpful to you. Try to write without editing, or even rereading. Write what comes. Make mistakes. Keep on writing. If you are more visual than verbal, you might try drawing.

As you fill the pages, you "add your light to the sum of lights," in Tolstoy's words. No one may know, except your family, close friends, the communion of saints, and God. That's a pretty good house. In keeping vigil, you follow a long tradition—and you make it your own.

The Vigil: Where and When

In the kitchen's stillness at dawn, in a hushed house late at night, and in a supermarket's long line, while holding a melon, you can keep vigil. In your study, your office cubicle, in a library's corner, you can wait on God. In the back of an empty church or garden, in a quiet museum or your laundry room, there is a place for vigil.

Andre Louf, a Trappist monk and scholar, suggests that you get up slightly earlier for your morning vigil, while it is quiet, and begin your day centered in God. Some sources suggest keeping vigil at fixed times, morning and evening. Another source suggests one fixed place. That could help; that could hinder. Perhaps a fixed time and place reinforce your commitment and honor the vigil. This is also a good way to build a steady routine, which, of course, is part of the discipline.

Some days, however, you may be traveling and you do your vigil on a plane; some days you may keep vigil when you arrive at work, other days before you leave the house. Again, what matters most is the vigil. Do whatever it is that helps you keep vigil and continue to keep it.

Tokens of Meaning
Often, people keep some meaningful token or objects nearby. What that might be, of course, varies from person to person, season to season. For me, at the moment, that means a small wooden cross; an island's stone; colored glass catching the sun; and often, as a focal point, a piece of fruit with a graceful shape. The cross and stone are gifts from two dear friends. The colored glass reminds me of church windows. Those associations, and many others, make an object more special, more significant. What would you bring to vigil time?

Answers may vary for you, from day to day, and that only brings more richness and flexibility into the vigil. You may bring a leaf, a shell, an icon, a crucifix, or a picture. Perhaps several items form a still life. Perhaps we simply offer our open hands. These details are helpful but should not dominate. The vigil itself is our true north.

Centered and Balanced
So it was for Noela N. Evans, author of *Meditations for the Passages and Celebrations of Life*. Her book grew from a period of bereavement, and to work through this hard time, she turned to the art of keeping vigil.

"I cannot promise that your vigils will make the hard times disappear, but I would remind you that your fully awakened presence is not only powerful, it can be magic," writes Evans.

After her mother's death, she had felt a need to "do something" other than grieve. We can relate to this; so often in depression, we wish we could do something other than being depressed. In many forms of depression, our thinking process is impaired and we cannot do many things, but we can keep vigil.

Evans kept vigil as she dealt with her loss and, as she writes, tried to recover her own balance. Every morning and evening, she set aside a special time for spiritual reading, silent reflection, and "waiting on God." As I did, she liked the continuity of keeping vigil, a fixed point, true north. In her grief, here is what vigils gave her: "The daily observance of the readings gave me a centeredness and a ritual that was a true comfort to my heart," she writes.

Centeredness. Comfort to the heart.

Much in demand, they are "true north."

A Mystery to Be Enjoyed

Settling into meditation can become your "true north." It is a discipline but not duty. It is a grace, not a work. Try not to grade yourself or your "progress." There is no number of steps to count, no prescribed order of doing things, no magic formula, no right or wrong.

Becoming still, centering, tuning in to the moment— each of these aspects can also be enjoyed. You may find that you feel clear and alive and at peace, at once. You may feel "nothing" in some meditations; that inner stillness is really "something." Try not to worry if your mind wanders. This is very common, especially at the beginning. Simply and gently return your attention to the moment or to your breathing.

"Life is a Mystery to be enjoyed, not a problem to be solved," says David Adam, rector of Lindisfarne. This wise saying is drawn from Celtic spirituality, but it applies to all. Perhaps we can try to see a *vigil* as a Mystery to be enjoyed, not a problem to be solved.

WAITING ON GOD

Spiritual guides have always recommended "waiting on God." The contemporary writer Richard Foster counsels: "[Let] those who find themselves devoid of the presence of God . . . wait on God. Wait, silent and still. Wait attentive and responsive. . . ." Trust in the character of God, who is always "out to do you good."

This practice seems mysterious to us today. We wonder: Are we waiting *for* God, for God's presence, or are we waiting and watching *with* God, waiting and watching in God's presence?

Waiting With Hope

The spirit's cry of hope is unforced prayer.

It is the *prayer we cannot help praying.*

Suppose your mind rules something out, giving sensible reasons, and all the while, your spirit is lifted in hope, hope that wells up naturally, unbidden, unforced. We see this with the disciples in the locked room. They are not impressed by news of the empty tomb; they refuse to believe Mary Magdalene's witness, and, yet, they stay, they hope—perhaps without realizing it. Our spirits cry out to God in hope, even as the mind goes on sensibly: give up, let go, move on. Sometimes our minds will contradict or completely ignore this—the spirit's cry of all cries. The spirit has its own voice, its own intuitive sense of our deepest needs. As we keep vigil, we will hear that inner voice more clearly.

Hope is a central element of the biblical vigil. Henri Nouwen wrote, "To wait on God is to anticipate the time that God will act," without presuming to tell God what to do and when. Instead, we trust that God knows our needs best. "Hope is based on the premise that the Other gives only what is good," he continued. "You put your unlimited trust in God who fulfills all promises."

Waiting with "hopeful expectancy" can be immensely useful in depression when we wait, and wait hard, to recover. If we wait on God for healing, we wait in hope; in Jesus, we know God's will for us is wholeness and healing. We center on God; we wait in hope.

Think of a man in late middle-age, mature and sensitive, who lived a single life in private, pained loneliness, voiced only in prayer. This man feared that he would grow old alone, without the loving marriage he had always wanted. He did something rather unusual about it, something unusual for these times. He kept a long vigil. His aunt, a devout Catholic, had a chronic illness she bore with unusual patience. She also kept vigils. They gave her great spiritual support—and impressed her nephew, who never forgot her and her spiritual practice.

The vigil helped this man bear his loneliness for years, stay on watch, and live with a sense of God's abiding presence. At last, he had a chance to meet a woman he had watched from a distance; someone who looked like a kindred spirit. His vigil practice had made him alert to grace and possibility. He offered up his hopes, his nerves, his dream in vigil. This gave him the courage to meet this woman, now his wife.

This story is not a Cinderella scenario. Cinderella did not keep vigils; she depended on chance and magic. This man's story is important for other reasons. First, it exemplifies a vigil of hope. This man lived in an openness to grace and in realism at the same time. Resignation and bitterness might have been easier, a kind of natural slide. Balanced and restrained hope can be hard work. The story also shows hope's power, particularly for people in depression.

Look at the power of hope in relation to Jesus' disciples, hiding out. They seem very close to letting hope go. Their hopelessness allowed their fear to take control.

By the time hopeful news came, they could not accept it, as we have seen. *Hope was resisted by the hopeless,* who seemed unable to recognize it. That is a disturbing situation for many reasons; here we simply address how powerful hope is. Its lack creates a locked room in our minds. Its presence frees us. When hope returned to the disciples, they were reborn.

Hopeful expectation, then, is important for us all. Hopelessness and depression make a particularly bad match. This is one of the reasons for telling the story of the man who hoped. It is a story that exemplifies what we might call the *"vigil spirit."*

This spirit does not focus on "results." It focuses on *God's continuous presence with us as we abide with a need, a longing,* a lost son or a long-term illness, which also may have long treatment phases. Depression is not brief, and often its treatment phase is not either. The vigil spirit goes the distance. Hope helps us to remain focused on the present. This way, we can avoid anxiety about the need to try out more than one medication, which is often necessary.

Waiting in Attentive Presence

Waiting on God is all about presence. We relate to God through focused presence, not words. Presence is at the heart of this "waiting." Presence is your way of being with God in vigil prayer. Presence is the vocabulary and the syntax of waiting on God. There are many doors into this kind of presence. Here are three that serve well:

First, remember a time when you have felt fully present to the moment: perhaps by the ocean or on a mountain, perhaps while you listened to music or talked with a very dear friend. It may happen for you when you watch the sun spill its light through stained glass or drench the sky with different colors as the day ends.

Frederick Buechner writes about a late winter afternoon when he was walking to a class he taught. As he walked, he saw a brilliant sunset beginning and, struck by it, he snapped out the lights in his classroom the moment he reached it. The room faced west and, in the dark, everything vanished but the sunset, framed by the windows. The teacher expected some laughter, some wise cracks. "But the astonishing thing was that the silence was as complete as you can get.... For over twenty minutes, nobody spoke a word."

Next, think of what you most love to do. What, for you, is a labor of love that completely absorbs you? What calls you to this intense concentration that cannot be forced, only welcomed—when the world falls away and you lose track of time? This happens to me sometimes when I write; it seems I just sat down at my desk and suddenly it's dinner time. How this happens seems miraculous, and it happens for all of us in some way, in some activity: as we run, swim, or sing; as we wrestle, paint, rebuild an engine, dance the tango, or study the stars.

"Where your treasure is, there your heart is also," Jesus tells us. Find your treasure and your heart and what it most loves. There you will find your way of being fully present—a way you can draw on, quite naturally, in the art of waiting on God.

A third door opens onto other people. Think of the people whose presence you cherish. Recall a time when that person's presence made a difference. No words need to be spoken; the person beside you was attentive, focused, *there*. Then imagine the opposite.

In his book *The Wounded Healer,* Henri Nouwen writes about the *power of presence.* There are many times when words quite literally fail, when presence is more powerful. Certain empty places within us can "never be filled with words but only by presence," he says, recounting a poignant story of a patient in counseling.

"Nothing and nobody is waiting for me," said this patient. This was significant, serious, and it had to be met the same way. Father Nouwen knew that could only be presence, a hand clasp, a look. Only then, Nouwen writes, "can the hope be born that there might be at least one exception . . . a hope that will make him whisper, 'Maybe, someone is waiting for me.' " In depression we need to hope in God.

Waiting with hope and waiting in attentive presence are fundamental to the practice of vigil keeping. They are, in a sense, attitudes that dispose us to the actual waiting. Now we look at eight ways to keep vigil.

The Silent Vigil

The first and most classic way of keeping vigil is focused, attentive silence as we wait for a sense of God's presence. This form is especially helpful if you have felt estranged or alienated from God or in times when God seems distant. There is no petition, no plea, no words at all. The stance is one of attentive presence to each moment, one of hopeful expectation. If you find such silence difficult, focus on your longing. Recall how deeply moved Jesus was as he traveled about Galilee, watching the people with compassion.

Sometimes, I think this form of "waiting on God" should be called *"waiting on ourselves."* God is always there, like the father waiting for the son to come down the road in the parable of the Prodigal Son. We are the ones who may wait a long time to take that road home. God's presence may come in the silent sound, in Christ's peace, in inexpressible ways.

Feeling nothing does not mean that nothing is happening. Our openness to God is, in itself, a happening.

It is response, always a response, to God's initiative. We are not opening the dialogue; we are only opening ourselves to what God has already begun, imperceptibly, invitationally, and, I believe, with unimaginable love.

If you do not feel estranged from God but have not given much time to God lately, you might go into a silent vigil and wait on a closer sense of God's presence. If you are already there, you may wait for a deepening of the relationship of "I and Thou," in Martin Buber's words.

The Vigil in the Present Moment

Another way of keeping vigil is a focused and intentional time of *being with God* in each moment of vigil. This is based on the thought of the great eighteenth-century mystic, Jean-Pierre de Caussade who developed the concept of the sacrament of the present moment. Each moment is a gift, and de Caussade encourages us to be present to God in every moment we can. A vigil is a way to do this. St. Catherine of Genoa also chose mindfulness of each moment in God's presence. "I will not worry myself with seeing beyond what God wants me to know. Instead, I abide in peace," she wrote.

The Vigil of Supplication

A third vigil form is *based on an intention. You* bring a special concern to this vigil, such as the healing of depression. As you bring a special object into a vigil, so you bring your intention with you into God's presence, as I bring my small wooden cross, stone, or piece of fruit. Without any spiritual nagging or pushing, you are simply waiting on God in your need. You are not pleading, not petitioning. You are waiting in hope and in trust for God's action in your life regarding your depression, and you wait attentively with a positive stance.

When a vigil is kept for someone in illness, we ask God to watch with us at the bedside. We see the pain in the light of God's presence. Now, as we begin vigils for ourselves or for others in depression, we ask God to watch with us in the depression. We trust God to abide with us in depressive illness and we rest in that trust. *In vigils, we abide with pain as we abide with God.*

The Thematic Vigil

Using a theme is a fourth way to keep vigil. Our theme might center on healing or relief from depressive illness. We saw how Noel Evans centered her vigil around her bereavement. In her book, she centers on other themes. Chapter 4 of this book contains several specially designed vigils to suit phases of depression, as well as "all purpose vigils" for any time, any need. I think this is the most helpful way to start out and to grow in the practice.

You can thread a vigil through your day with a technique called "breath prayer." Take a line from your morning vigil's reading, and keep it in your mind and think of it now and then, recalling its essence, recalling the peace of your vigil time. The line is used somewhat as a mantra once was, in a different practice.

Select the phrase for its meaning and also for length—short enough to say with one breath, perhaps eight syllables for so, although this is flexible. You might also take a phrase from your own prayers and use it throughout the day. For example, "Lord Jesus, please heal me."

Breath prayer comes quietly into your day, to hear in your mind when you wish. Associated with the Russian Orthodox Church, the practice follows the biblical mandate to "pray without ceasing." The most famous breath prayer is the "Jesus Prayer" from the Orthodox tradition: "Lord Jesus Christ, son of the living God, have mercy on me, a sinner." This is sometimes assumed to be the breath prayer; in fact, this can take any form you wish. Breath prayer is personal, informal, reminding you of God's presence and care.

Struggle as Vigil

Struggle is yet another way to keep vigil. Sometimes we feel like Jacob, wrestling throughout the night with the angel of the Lord. Spiritual directors often see these soul struggles as a positive sign of engaged presence and authentic relationship with God. They show that we care enough to enter the struggle. Apathy in the spiritual life, not struggle, is the real danger sign.

We may enter a vigil of struggle because of an external situation that challenges us and surrounds us. At other times, we struggle within ourselves, feeling conflicted and ambivalent; then the struggle rises within from our core. Or perhaps we struggle with some spiritual anguish, some guilt or regret, or anger at God who, we believe, does not care. We may even see God as our adversary, the one with whom we struggle, and to whom we are unwilling to give over our lives. We hold on, afraid to let go. All such shrug-goes can be factors in depression; they can also be good material for a vigil.

In a masterful essay, "The Magnificent Defeat", from the book of the same name, Frederick Buechner writes of the crafty Jacob, wrestling throughout the night with the angel of the Lord. Jacob must learn that his worldly cunning has made him materially rich but spiritually impoverished. He struggles, he thrashes, he wrestles with God over this. Success, in the world's terms, is something we can win on our own, but we need more: peace and love and wholeness are gifts that come only from God. Jacob struggles with this through a long night before he understands love as God's gift.

The soul's struggle can become more than blind thrashing; it can be focused into a vigil. The readings and prayers we choose may help us focus on the crux of the matter. Perhaps we are angry; some of the psalmists were angry as well. We can let a psalm shape our vigil. Through selected readings and reflections, we give our feelings a voice, a name, an outlet. As we do, in the midst of struggle, like others before us, we find God.

Vigils in Times of Turmoil

Struggles are tough. Turmoil is tougher. Certainly we would not expect to encounter God in life's messiness. Depression is messy. Anxiety is messy. Depressive Hurmoil is *very* messy. Does God step into our turbulence? The example of Jesus is always before us, affirming that God does. Even so, there are times when God does not seem close, especially when we are in turmoil.

As a hospital chaplain-intern, I heard so many people say that they thought God was "too busy" to hear their prayers. To them, quite literally, God was "above it all," the unmoved mover, impassive, remote. God greets us with chill formality: No scenes, please. No outbursts. Chin up. Stay on-message. Speak up. Keep it short.

This is not the Judeo-Christian understanding of God. This is not the image of God shown to us in Jesus "moved by pity"—pity as *heed,* loving-kindness and compassion. Jesus weeps at the grave of his friend Lazarus and over Jerusalem. Once there, at the Temple, Jesus acted in his righteous anger: He upset the tables of the money-changers and drove the traders from the Temple.

Jesus, unlike his cousin, the austere John the Baptist, also came to dinners and weddings; he joked that the Son of Man might be called a glutton and a drunkard. After the last supper of his earthly life, after the last table fellowship he would know, we see rising turmoil again in

Jesus, at Gethsemane. This is quite an emotional range for the holy one who says, "Whoever has seen me has seen the Father" (John 14:9). Clearly, then, turmoil does not preclude God's presence. Turmoil is another way to keep vigil.

Certainly, the disciples of Jesus we saw at the beginning of this chapter were in turmoil. They were frightened, ashamed, and shocked. Perhaps they were also angry and resentful, doubting Jesus and his big promises—turmoil again. Once again, into the turmoil comes the risen Christ. It may not be what we expect, but *turmoil is a place where we wait on and encounter God.*

Vigils, then, encompass more than we had first thought. They can be serene, silent prayer, calm attentiveness, or something less neat, less presentable in polite society. Vigils can start with a yowl of pain, not a demure "Ahem." They can be about fear and lost nerve and anger. They can be about lament.

Vigils of Lament

We cry out to God in depression; we may cry out silently most of the day. When we cry out to God in prayer, no matter how pained we feel, we are joining a long and honored tradition.

Vigils of lament are rooted in real life, raw emotion, and in those great wails of prayer, the psalms. How well we understand this form if we have depression. A friend of mine found the psalms very important to her in a depressive episode. She, like many of us, may have kept "vigils of lament" without naming them. Anyone in depression knows lament in a negative way.

The psalmists see it differently, paradoxically, perhaps, once again. In the psalms, emotional distress is never scorned as an unworthy offering. Quite the opposite. We are invited to *bring our full range of emotion to God,* excluding neither anguish nor gratitude.

"The psalmist understands that nothing human is foreign to God, and that nothing under heaven is off limits to the prayers of God's people," writes Michael Jinkins in his superb book *In the House of the Lord:* "The psalms of lament . . . refuse to allow us to rush to a happy ending. They insist that we give expression to our human sorrows and sufferings and present all of them to God."

In some depressions, there is weeping, sometimes uncontrollable weeping, or we lament our lives, mistakes, failures, and losses. We cannot think of anything else. Regret is a cousin to lament, but regret sounds more acceptable, more restrained, more adult.

Lament makes us uncomfortable. Lament embarrasses us. Worst of all, in our culture, *lament is not cool.* We are obsessed with being cool, having cool, keeping our cool, so we tend to relate lamentation to self-serving theatrics or obnoxious whining. Secretly, we regard it as weakness. "Don't be a crybaby," we are cautioned early on, and that is one injunction we remember. The line between lament and whining seems to blur.

Psalmist and psychologist agree. We have noted the negative role of repressed emotions. If your personal vigil is one of lament, it is confirmed by ancient *and* modern wisdom. If you are crying out to God, your voice joins a chorus of God's people.

Vigils of Devotion

An eighth type of vigil is the vigil of devotion. In our most private, personal vigils we may watch and wait for long periods, completely unknown to others. In such vigils, we allow ourselves to be vulnerable, to open our very selves and our deepest needs to God. This may take courage at first, as a new level of trust develops.

"You have to keep going back to the source: God's love for you," Henri Nouwen wrote. We are easy and open with one who loves us, more guarded with others, even in a subtle way. God's love for us is the starting place for all vigils. "Give your agenda to God," he suggests. Keep on giving it, every day, to start or end a vigil, whether we are keeping vigil ourselves or as intercession for others.

Sometimes a loved one's depression can be very hard to bear. Since depression strikes at the core of the self, the loved one may seem distant.

Progress may be slow and frustrating; supportive friends and family begin to feel helpless. They may not realize how valued they are.

William Styron, in *Darkness Visible,* writes about the loving support of his wife, which made a great difference in his depression and recovery. This kind of support really matters. I hope that material from this chapter, indeed, this book, can offer some support to supporters. Vigils of devotion, described here, are ideal for friends and families of people in depression.

There are many times when all we can do is pray. We cannot "fix" whatever is wrong. We cannot "do" anything. We can only "be"—and wait. We can be with the situation in spirit. A vigil of devotion gives needed support to us in this spiritual labor of love.

This devotion gives energy to our prayer, reflection, and waiting on God. You may be praying as the parent of a child in trouble, or for a spouse in depression, or for a parent whose health is failing. In each case, you love the other one and at the same time your love may bring you pain, but a vigil of devotion can be a way to cope with that pain, as we sit with it in the presence of God.

"Do not hesitate to love and love deeply," Nouwen encourages us. "When your love is truly giving . . . those whom you love will not leave your heart even when they depart. . . . Those you have loved deeply become a part of you." This sense of continuity with the loved one is mirrored in the continuity of the vigil practice, day by day, evening by evening. In those times just before sleep and just after waking, the loved one's name can be given over to God, very simply, as you start your day or night.

Vigils of devotion can bring special comfort to those in the all-important support system. Often, depressions worsen in isolation, where suicidal thoughts can gain power, but if seriously depressed persons know that their lives matter to someone, they can hang on and keep working with the depression. Family and friends may also appreciate the daily vigil practice for its continuity, a supportive factor in itself. An intercessor therefore *keeps vigil with God for the depressed person.* As you offer your attentive presence to God, you and your loved one are held in God's love.

There is a sense of continuity in the vigil way that suits all kinds of situations. It is a spirituality that one could practice for a lifetime, on a continuing basis. This was the case with Elizabeth, a mother of two grown sons, a woman with friends and health, a good job, a good life. No one knew of her devout spiritual life, and no one knew that she had been keeping vigil for ten years. This vigil was for her younger son, deeply depressed but unwilling to face it and now far from home. At daily Mass and throughout each day, Elizabeth kept a regimen of prayer and reflection, a practice which also helped her cope with this difficult situation, this absent son. For her, this was more than intercessory prayer. This was an ongoing vigil and a mother's constant watch, with God, through God, over her son. This was *a vigil of devotion;* Mary, the mother of Jesus, must have kept such vigils for Jesus, throughout his life.

We may presume that we lack patience for such vigils—until some news comes, some danger looms, touching someone we love, or perhaps something appears on the edges of our lives and taps our deepest longings. During the final events of Jesus' life, his mother was helpless. There was nothing she could do to protect her son. She appears briefly in John's gospel at the cross. I imagine her in seclusion, devoting all her energies to intercession. Although she could do nothing overtly to protect her son, she could do much in prayer and private vigil at this intensely personal time.

THE ONE WHO ALWAYS WATCHES

We have seen that a vigil is a spiritual way to abide with depression. The personal vigil is accessible to us consistently, every day, in most seasons of the soul, in most situations.

How this happens is no mystery.

It all has to do with our intentionality. We can choose to open a time or situation up to God. We can invite God into our depression, into our waiting, our lament and turmoil, our devotion and hope—and God is there, watching for us, waiting outside our locked doors.

Our locked doors?

We know the truth of it: We know we are in that locked room in Jerusalem; we are with those disciples in their dim hideout. Often, so often, we inhabit that upper room with the gray light and the air that is perfumed with silence, and the men, the disciples, waiting there. Sometimes it's hard to distinguish ourselves from them:

Eleven men in one room for three days, in despair and in fear. There is no hope to be seen—and yet it is there, small as a dust mote, refusing to leave. It must be there, or the disciples would be gone from the city, by stealth, by night, by now. If the place is so dangerous, if these men are so imperiled, why do they stay around?

Why, then, do they stay?

They are waiting for something they cannot name, something unspoken; they cannot explain. There is that fine dusting of hope in them—hope that has slipped to them, spilled into them like rain, like blood, like grains of wheat. They don't know what it is, but they stay; they wait.

Then it happens. Somehow, a stranger gets into their room. No one has knocked. No one remembers unlocking the door. No one remembers leaving it open, and yet, he got in, this cloaked stranger; there he stands, his mantle drawn up over his head, his face in shadow. For an instant no one can move. In that instant, he speaks.

"Peace be with you," says the stranger.

That is the voice they know and would know always and yet such things cannot be. He lets his mantle slip back and now in the light they see his face. They scarcely breathe, waiting for him to vanish into the still evening air, and as they gaze at him, they mistrust their wits and their sight and their hearing

Is this a spirit? But he breathes, gives off warmth; his eyes are lit and alive. Now, as they look at his face, perhaps their own eyes fill, glimmering, but perhaps it is only a trick of the light. Perhaps it is only a trick of the light that this man so resembles him, so exactly, solid and real, standing among them and smiling, not angry. Perhaps it is only a trick of the light. Perhaps.

But they know it is not.

They know it before they hear his voice again, that voice, his and no other, as once more Jesus says to them all, "Peace be with you."

■

FOUR

VIGILS FOR TIMES OF
DEPRESSION

Consider the lilies

They grow wild and white in a field. The afternoon sun, slanting through them, turns them to flame: a thousand vigil lights for your prayers. The field is in Galilee —or wherever you happen to be. God offers you a field of lilies, ablaze but not burnt, as a sign to you; an invitation to keep vigil.

Consider the field as the place for your vigils, a field to uphold you and strengthen you in depression. Here you find inspiration. You find firm ground for support as you watch and wait and abide. Our spirits need a field such as this. In depression, we need it more. A century ago, mill workers, desolate and poor, sang: "Hearts starve as well as bodies. ... Give us bread but give us roses, too." Jesus gives us bread—and lilies.

Now, as we turn to the actual practice of vigil-keeping, we might keep that field in mind. We have used images that take depression seriously, as it deserves—catacombs, wilderness, Golgotha, a locked room. Now, we come to an open and spacious place. This is where we start our new approach to depression.

In the following material, you will find a variety of vigil plans to try, perhaps to make a part of each day. You are invited to adjust or embellish any vigil you like; the forms are flexible. Depression, we know, has different phases and different degrees. Such variations are addressed here with vigils of hope and lament, vigils for progress and setbacks. There is no right or wrong order to these vigils; you are likely to try them as they fit your needs at the time.

All of these vigils are designed for individual or group use. If you have a prayer partner or prayer group, any of these vigils would apply. If you choose to keep vigil on an individual basis, the vigils are a good fit. As you work with them, you may want to refer back to Chapter 3's discussion of "waiting on God," or you may simply choose to begin and let the form lead you.

Almost everything you need for your vigils is here, in this book. Texts of a psalm, a poem, and most readings are reproduced here. Occasionally, you will need a bible, candles, perhaps a cherished object or two, and, in one case, a photo. All of these are strictly optional. This book allows you to focus on the vigil, not its props. The one "extra" you will need is a notebook to serve as your journal. I use the black and white speckled copy books from the drug store—a minor investment.

After you have grown used to keeping vigil, you might want to create your own. The "Vigil Plans" in this chapter may provide you with a basis for your own vigil designs. Among the vigils offered here, you may find one that works well for you, that you may want to continue beyond a day or two or even a week. If that happens, you can use the particular vigil on an open-ended basis, simply taking a longer, deeper look at the readings and questions for reflection.

As you keep vigil, you will want to avoid interruptions. Your voice mail or answering machine can take messages while you turn off the phone. Your spouse or children would surely respect your vigil times. If you set an alarm clock to end your vigil, find one that makes a gentle sound. If you are aware of miscellaneous sounds during vigil, just let them flow by like sticks in a stream, observed but not engaged, as suggested by a seasoned spiritual guide.

Place

Where will you be keeping your vigils? You have already thought of that, most likely. You are the best judge of vigil locales that suit your situation. Generally, a quiet room at home is most convenient. Other places could be an empty church, a quiet library, your own basement or garage. In nice weather, *a safe* park or garden might appeal to you. Some people can even keep vigil while traveling.

Logistics work out. The vigil begins. It becomes your focus. Wherever you keep vigil, wherever you offer time to God, whether the setting is a laundry room or a littered basement, that is a place of encounter with God—and that is holy ground. Perhaps you may never keep vigil in a park or a garden or a field. Even so:

Timing

Be flexible about the exact time of day and the amount of time you spend on each part.

• Take a few minutes to settle yourself and begin.

• Allow five to ten minutes for reading and reflection.

• Take another five to ten minutes if you are writing in your journal.
• Allow five minutes for quiet, simply waiting on God using the breath prayer.
• Allow five to ten minutes for ending with personal prayer, in conversation with God or using a prayer you know by heart.

Breath Prayer

In each vigil a form of prayer called breath prayer is suggested. This is a form of prayer that Christians have used for centuries. Paying attention to our breathing helps to settle us and screen out the distractions around us. A word or phrase is suggested, but you should feel free to choose another if that works better for you. In one vigil, for example, the phrase, "In your light, I see light" is suggested. As you breathe in, you would say to yourself, "In your light." As you breathe out, you would say, "I see light." If the phrase is too long for recitation in one breath, extend it over two. If this practice is new to you, it may seem awkward at first, but if you give it time, it can gradually become a helpful way to pray.

Consider the lilies.

"Do not be anxious," Jesus says, glancing beyond his listeners, gazing at a field of wild flowers. "If you know how to give good gifts, how much more will your Father in heaven give good things to those who ask?" (Matthew 7:11). We ask to be led into vigil.

We ask. We hesitate. We try. Only then do we realize that God has been watching for us, waiting for us at a field spilling over with lilies, glowing like vigil lights in the sun. God has watched and waited from the beginning. How did we get the idea that vigils were *our* invention?

Father, forgive.

You wait for us, first, last, and always. When we join the vigil at last, you are there.

1. GETTING THROUGH THE DAY . . . WITH A PSALM OF LAMENT

It stretches ahead, this time of depression; we occupy it like uneasy renters on an uncertain lease. Each day we hope to pack up and leave. Each day we stay on, by necessity rather than choice. Each day seems long, empty, and bleak. There may be pain, there may be numb resignation, that sense of being half-alive. How do we get through such days? Give depression a voice—a psalm of lament.

"My God, my God, why have you forsaken me?" With this cry from the cross, Jesus opens the psalms of lament to us in a new way. He has prayed this first line of Psalm 22. These words are personal. They are not a sign of lost faith. They cry out for us when we cannot cry out ourselves, when despair silences us.

"Jesus Christ shows us that a cry of lament— however harsh—is not something outside the faith.... Indeed, lamentation of the most profound, and profoundly human sort, has been assumed by God in Christ," writes Michael Jinkins. Even when we feel abandoned, we pray, and through Jesus, crying out on the cross, we can understand lament as congruent with faith. Here is another of God's great paradoxes, like the silent sound and the death that is life—lament as a form of authentic faith and honest communion with God.

In Jesus, God enters and participates in our suffering right to the end and to great depth. The "crucified God" is with us in lament, fully and deeply, in a costly way. If we can think of God as participating in our suffering, our sense of "God-forsakenness" lessens. We are not alone as we cry out from the mazes and deserts and locked rooms of life. As we cry out, particularly in the psalms of lament, in our own jagged voices, we hear God's.

Notes

1. In preparation, read the psalm through once for overview.
2. The most important thing about timing is simply this: showing up. Keep the discipline of morning, noon, and evening. You will get more out of it as you go along. The psalm's structure also structures your day, dividing it into smaller units. The units can be smaller still if you choose, by reading the psalm in smaller segments, or rereading it with added reflections for mid-morning, mid-afternoon, and last thing at night.
3. You may find it helpful to create a ritual to accompany your prayer. Some suggestions:

   • Light a candle for each vigil segment.

   • Select a few objects that have meaning for *you and* for this vigil theme. Focus on a different one in each vigil segment, adding a few minutes of extra reflection.

   • If you do light a candle in each segment, you may find one candle burning down as you light a new one, or the candle light may overlap. This can be another focal point for reflection, if you so choose. If you need to leave a candle, put it out and relight when you return.

Vigil Plan

Morning

   • Brief opening prayer, offering this time to God.
   • Psalm 13:1-2. Read and reflect on the psalm verses and the commentary.

- Write your own petition, one line or word.
- Breath prayer: one word or phrase from you or the psalm, suggested phrase: "Grief in my heart."
- Conclude with your own prayer.

Midday
- Brief opening prayer, offering this time to God.
- Psalm 13:2-3. Read and reflect on the psalm verses and the commentary.
- Write your own petition, one line or word.
- Breath prayer: one word/phrase from you or the psalm, suggested phrase: "Give light to my eyes."
- Conclude with your own prayer.

Evening
- Brief opening prayer, offering this time to God.
- Psalm 13:4-5. Read and reflect on the psalm verses and the commentary.
- Write your own petition, one line or word.
- Breath prayer: one word or line from you or the psalm, suggested phrase: "Your saving help."
- Conclude with your own prayer.

Psalm 13
[Lament]
(1) How long, 0 Lord?
Will you forget me forever?
(2) How long will you hide your face from me?
How long do I lay up counsel in my mind, and grief in my heart, day after day?

[Petition]
(3) Look upon me and answer me, 0 Lord my God; give light to my eyes, lest I sleep in death,

(4) Lest my enemy say, "I have prevailed over him," And my foes rejoice that I have fallen.

[Statement of confidence/trust]
(5) But I put my trust in your mercy; my heart is joyful because of your saving help.
(6) I will sing to the Lord, for he has dealt with me richly; I will praise the Name of the Lord Most High.

Commentary
In depression, we cannot avoid the valley of the shadow, but we have God's assurance: we are not there alone; we are not left there forever. Neither are we left in the valley of forgetfulness that begins Psalm 13. This is a psalm of "individual lament," presented for a person who is ill and who fears abandonment by God.

As noted earlier, the psalm moves from "lament" in verses one and two, into "petition" in verses three and four, and finally in verses five and six to a "statement of confidence and trust in God." This is the classic structure we use to format this vigil and can apply to many others.

"How long," we cry with the psalmist: "a biblical formula for fright and exasperation," writes James Luther Mays, who sees verse two as a way of saying, "How long must I keep learning from my pain?" This is often the way we feel when we are told emotional pain is a learning experience.

Then there is a more direct exclamation: "Look! Answer me!" (verses 3-4). We may think this is the cry of a child in a tantrum, but it means quite literally what it says. It *invites God to look at us and into us,* through and through, and see the depth of our need. This plea to be seen, to be fully known by God, is daring and vulnerable at the same time.

"Give light to my eyes" is to be read as a tender plea for life rather than death, and most of all to God who sustains us, even when we do not experience it. The reference to God's saving help in verse five is a reference to *heed*. The word expresses a divine attribute, the quality of loving-kindness without measure, compassion, grace, and mercy.

The psalm's threefold structure, as noted earlier, divides the day into smaller units, speaks to you where you are, and offers you a way to cry out to God. At the end of the day, if you record your personal lament in your journal, you will have written your own psalm, one you may want to work with further or leave, dated, to mark your progress.

Other Psalms of Lament for your use:

Psalms *3-17*, except *8* and *9;*

Psalms *22-28*, except *24;*

Psalms *31, 35-43, 47, 51-64*, except *60;*

Psalms *69, 71, 73, 86, 88, 102, 109*, and 130.

2. A VIGIL FOR A TIME OF IMPROVEMENT OR RECOVERY

You are almost afraid to admit it, as if your "improvement" might vanish if you speak its name. When asked how you are, you may say, "Urn, well, not too bad ... I think, maybe, for now," instead of "FINE!!" You knock wood and mutter a prayer, then hold your breath. As the day goes on, as you do more than you could do yesterday, the day or the week before, you don't take this for granted. You don't take a lot of things for granted now

Throughout the day, you keep listening to your inner self. This is not narcissism. This is keeping your eye on the road. This is listening to the sound of the engine, alert to that soft knocking noise, that faint hesitation on hills, those cues you heard before. Such vigilance is not at all baseless. Most depressions run in cycles. More often than not, depressions recur, and so we are not overreacting if we feel better but cautious, grateful but guarded. How do we offer thanks to God in this state of caution? How do we avoid poisoning our progress with fear? How do we accept the gift and open it, wear it and bless it, knowing it may not last? These are important questions for people with chronic or recurrent depression. I understand the ambiguity of such times of improvement. We are always learning more about seizing the day, living the moment, even as we remain realistic about depression's patterns.

Here is a vigil that offers one possibility, one answer.

Notes

1. I see this vigil in two formats. The first is *a vigil in three segments of one day:* morning, noon, and evening. The second format would be to keep it over the course of *three days,* in two segments per day, morning and evening.
2. This vigil is anchored in the poem "Welcome Morning" by Anne Sexton, a gifted American poet (1928-1974). Acclaimed in her time, she struggled with emotional illness (far more severe than depression) for most of her life. Her poem shows gratitude in a time of improvement in illness. She shows—but does not tell—how thanksgiving to God, in the moment, in life's details, offsets fear of losing the gift which lives when it is shared. In preparation read "Welcome Morning" through once, as an overview.
3. Decide in advance how much time to allot for each segment.

Vigil Plan

For a one-day vigil.

Morning
- Brief opening prayer, offering this time to God.
- Read and reflect on stanza one (set off by a space break) and the commentary following the poem.
- In your journal, consider one of the questions for reflection or reflect on your own.
- Breath prayer: select a word or phrase from your writing or from the poem.
- Finish with your own prayer.

Midday
- Brief opening prayer, offering this time to God.
- Read and reflect on stanza two and the commentary following the poem.
- In your journal, consider one of the questions for reflection or reflect on your own.
- Breath prayer: select a word or phrase from your writing or from the poem.
- Finish with your own prayer.

Evening
- Brief opening prayer, offering this time to God.
- Read and reflect on stanza three and the commentary following the poem.
- In your journal, consider one of the questions for reflection or reflect on your own.
- Breath prayer: select a word or phrase from your writing or from the poem.
- Finish with your own prayer.

Plan for a Three-Day Vigil
- Keep two vigil times per day, morning and evening.
- Follow the steps outlined above for each day, using one stanza for each day.

"Welcome Morning" by Anne Sexton

> There is joy in all:
> in the hair I brush each morning
> in the Cannon towel, newly washed,
> that I rub my body with each morning,
> in the chapel of eggs I cook
> each morning,
> in the outcry from the kettle
> that heats my coffee
> each morning,
> in the spoon and chair
> that cry "hello there, Anne,"
> each morning,
> in the godhead of the table
> that I set my silver, plate, cup upon
> each morning.
>
> All this is God,
> right here in my pea-green house
> each morning
> and I mean,
> though I often forget,
> to give thanks,
> to faint down by the kitchen table
> in a prayer of rejoicing
> as the holy birds at the kitchen window
> peck into their marriage of seeds.

So while I think of it,
let me paint a thank-you on my palm
for this God, this laughter of the morning,
lest it go unspoken.
The Joy that isn't shared, I've heard,
Dies young.

Commentary

There is abundant thanksgiving in the Bible. In the Old Testament, there are texts of thanksgiving too numerous to name, such as the "Song of Hannah" (see page 121), gratitude after the Exodus, in addition to many psalms and feasts of thanksgiving to God.

In Hebrew, the word for *thanks* "basically means praise and only derivatively does it express gratitude," writes James L. Mays. "In giving thanks, Israel is only responding with praise to what Yahweh does," in creation, in history, and for Israel. God is the initiator. Thanks, then, is *response* to God, and that *response is praise.* In the New Testament, the Christian is *never to pray without giving thanks* for what God has done for the individual, Paul asserts in many passages (Phil. 4:6, 2 Corinthians, and 1 Timothy). The Greek word "eucharist," of course, means thanksgiving. Literally, it combines the word that simultaneously means "good" and "true" with the root *charis,* meaning "grace."

Thus, as Christians, our central sacrament is thanksgiving, true grace, in word and act, for what God has done for us in Jesus Christ. We also give thanks for the Incarnation with the Blessed Virgin Mary, whose Magnificat is one of the best-known biblical songs of praise. As in the Old Testament, there are too many texts to cite, but all *thanksgiving is response to God in Christ.*

(Note: This is not homework. Questions for reflection follow, but don't try to do them all unless you truly want to do so and have time. If you are doing this as a one-day vigil, just take one or two questions from each section. If you do this as a three-day vigil, each day you can do more.)

This poem shows us how to thank God for the present moment and see grace in the so-called "small" details of everyday life. We can remember when depression robbed us of simple joys, when nothing seemed to matter. Now, after emerging from illness, everything matters: "There is joy in all."

Stanza One

Eggs, kettle, coffee, spoon—all are signs of God's grace, the "glory in the ordinary," as expressed in Celtic spirituality. The "simple" joys are related to God in the metaphors of stanza one: the "chapel of eggs," the "godhead of the table," and the liturgical rhythm of the words, "each morning," like a chant connecting the images.

Try reading this stanza aloud and listen to the chant-like rhythm it makes. Each morning, God is revealed in the homely details of breakfast—if we look for God there, if we see with the eyes of grace and faith. There are eucharistic overtones when Sexton refers to silver, plate, cup, set on "the godhead of the table,"—chalice and paten. Every meal, she suggests, is almost sacramental, almost like eucharist if it is seen as thanksgiving to God.

Questions for Reflection on Stanza One

1. When you feel an improvement in depression, which everyday details of your life seem graced? Sacramental? Where do you see "God's glory in the ordinary"?

2. Create a simple scene like this one in your mind and add a repeated chant, as Sexton does with "each morning." What scenes come to mind? What

"chant"? What settings or situations evoke your gratitude to God for improvement in depression?
3. We saw that the biblical view of thanksgiving is seen as response to God. To what blessings does Sexton respond? Is her chanted refrain, "each morning," yet another "thank you"? Is she expressing gratitude for each morning itself?
4. This is a strong example of being in the moment, seeing each moment as holy, praising God for each moment. When and how do such moments come to you?

Stanza Two

"All this is God," the poet goes on, confirming our sense of the first stanza. "All this is God" related to the first lines of stanza one, "There is joy in all." In all these homely joys, there is God's grace, and this happens each morning, repeated again, but we forget to give thanks, the poem admits. Respite from illness makes all new, so wondrous, we want to kneel at the kitchen table, which again seems like an altar. Even the birds are holy, when we look with God's sight, at the creation God made and found "good." In this stanza, notice how the circle of holy joy widens. In stanza one we have the indoor world of grace. Now we move to the outdoor world and its nearest creatures, also breakfasting with joy in the outside world.

Questions for Reflection on Stanza Two
1. How does improvement in depression make you feel newly grateful? When you feel better, what do you say in a prayer of rejoicing?
2. How can we keep this kind of gratitude when we feel better more often? Can we cultivate thanksgiving as part of spiritual practice?

3. Where is a holy place for you at home? Where is your table-altar?

Stanza Three

Now the circle of grace and gratitude widens even more. The poet wants to paint a "thank-you" on her palm for God. On God's palms, our names are written, according to the prophet Isaiah. God says, "See, upon the palms of my hands, I have written your name" (Isaiah 49:16). This is one of God's many expressions of love. Now the poet turns the image around and *openly* thanks God by offering her palm. On it she wants to write thanks, "good grace," eucharist—words in Greek that signify God's presence through God's grace. Again, we respond to God's initiative.

God is in "this laughter of the morning." There is, however, a warning note at the end of this poem. Perhaps only someone with serious intermittent illness could capture the joy—and the warning. This joy is so very precious. It is as rare as the pearl in Jesus' parable. God comes to us as joy, but we may not always notice. We may not see clearly in illness. All the more reason to give thanks now, this moment, and not put it off. We keep joy by giving it. We lose joy by keeping it. Once again, in the words of Paul Tillich, "paradox is logical," certainly with God.

The joy that isn't shared dies young. Holy joy is meant to be shared, as is the eucharist, as is thanks. We cannot hoard these times of grace and glory. We can only note them, share them, spend them. All the more important, then, to give thanks for the One who is always there, but seen and praised best when we are getting well.

Questions for Reflection on Stanza Three

1. Would it be meaningful to you to ink a thank-you to God on your palm? If not, how would you offer a similar special sign of thanks?
2. Our names are written on God's palm. Why is this meaningful, do you think? Why would an ancient prophet and a modern poet use this image? (There is no right answer; just a matter for reflection.) We work with our hands, we need our hands, and our hands are almost always visible to us. Is that part of the reason?
3. Henri Nouwen once told a story about a woman who clutched a coin tightly in her hand, afraid to give it up. She served as an image of the attitude we sometimes have toward God. Imagine yourself with such a clenched fist and then imagine yourself with an open hand. This may be a helpful image for you in meditation: opening your hand, offering your hand to God.
4. Think about the sense of warning at the end of the poem. Do we express thanks to God in the moment, as we feel it? How do we share thanksgiving and joy with God? What would you write on your palm?

3. A VIGIL OF LIGHT

This is an all-purpose vigil, less scripted or guided than others, to leave you a space for your own reflections and prayer. You might use this vigil "when words fail," when you feel too muted, too drained for verbal expression. At such times, images may be better than words. You may also use this vigil when you want lots of room for prayer around a theme, such as this one. Also, after you become more practiced at keeping vigil, you may want to design your own; here is a basic form you might use.

Notes
1. You may want to use an oil lamp, a candle, or another light to accompany your prayer.
2. If your weather is sunny, try putting a colored bottle or jar in a sunny window and watch the light that comes through.

Vigil Plan
A seven-day vigil, kept on consecutive days:

Day One
- In the morning, read and reflect on John 8:12.
- In the evening, read and reflect on John 1:5.
- In your journal, consider one of the reflection questions that follow or simply write your own thoughts.
- Breath prayer: one word or phrase from the passage or "In your light, I see light."
- Finish with your own prayer.

Day Two
- In the morning, read and reflect on Luke 8:16.
- In the evening, read and reflect on Luke 11:36.
- In your journal, consider one of the reflection questions that follow or simply write your own thoughts.
- Breath prayer: one word or phrase from the passage or "In your light, I see light."
- Finish with your own prayer.

Day Three
- In the morning, read and reflect on Luke 15:8.

- In the evening, read and reflect on Luke 15:9.
- In your journal, consider one of the reflection questions that follow or simply write your own thoughts.
- Breath prayer: one word or phrase from the passage or "In your light, I see light."
- Finish with your own prayer.

Day Four
- In the morning, read and reflect on Luke 1:78.
- In the evening, read and reflect on Luke 1:79.
- In your journal, consider one of the reflection questions that follow or simply write your own thoughts.
- Breath prayer: one word or phrase from the passage or "In your light, I see light."
- Finish with your own prayer.

Day Five
- In the morning, read and reflect on Mark 10:51-52.
- In the evening, read and reflect on Luke 24:29.
- In your journal, consider one of the reflection questions that follow or simply write your own thoughts.
- Breath prayer: one word or phrase from the passage or "In your light, I see light."
- Finish with your own prayer.

Day Six
- In the morning, read and reflect on Acts 2:2-3.
- In the evening, read and reflect on Exodus 3:1-12.
- In your journal, consider one of the reflection questions that follow or simply write your own thoughts.

- Breath prayer: one word or phrase from the passage or "In your light, I see light."
- Finish with your own prayer.

Day Seven
- In the morning, read and reflect on Genesis 1:1-4.
- In the evening, read and reflect on Matthew 2:9.
- In your journal, consider one of the reflection questions that follow or simply write your own thoughts.
- Breath prayer: one word or phrase from the passage or "In your light, I see light."
- Finish with your own prayer.

Commentary

In the Judeo-Christian tradition, light is a symbol of God, the presence of the holy, and spiritual illumination. In Genesis, the creation of the world is begun with God's creation of light. God's countenance is light, and to God, even the darkness is not night (Psalm 4:6, Psalm 139). Salvation history is often marked with light and fire. Adam and Eve are expelled from Eden by an angel with a flaming sword. The call of Moses comes through a miraculously burning bush, and God's self-revelation on Sinai is set off by a great display of fire and light.

In the New Testament, a heavenly light guides the shepherds, first visitors to the Christ child. Jesus, as God's son, is "light from light" and "the light of the world." He uses the imagery of light in many of his teachings. His revelation of his divine sonship in the transfiguration involves supernatural light, as does one announcement of Christ's resurrection, from an angel who resembles lightning.

Darkness has opposite connotations—death, evil, and danger. However, as the gospel of John makes clear, the darkness can never overcome the light, which is life, both of which are of God.

Questions for Reflection
1. Where do you locate light in your own life?
2. How does light symbolize the holy for you, if at all?
3. How did a bonfire or hearth fire support life prior to electricity?
4. Do you associate depression with darkness? Do you associate light with wellness?
5. If light is a powerful symbol for you of the holy, of prayer, or of well-being, how can you use this symbolism more often?
6. Light actually has mild anti-depressant properties. Psycho-pharmacologists recommend at least twenty minutes of sunlight a day. As noted earlier, some people find help from light boxes. Can you find a way to get more physical light into your life?
7. What does light symbolize for you? Life? Reason? Hope? Christ? Revelation?

4. A VIGIL FOR DESPAIR, WHEN WORDS FAIL

Images sometimes help us more than words. At times in depression, our inner pain and hopelessness are too strong for verbal expression. Other times, we are simply exhausted from trying, from hoping, from the depression itself. One of depression's features is difficulty with concentration and complex thinking.

Here is a vigil that can be used in times of *despair* and anguish—or in times of peace and *wellness*. The timing is flexible. It could be a one-day or one-week vigil, or longer if you wish. Consider this, also, as a once-a-week vigil, perhaps on Sundays, to set apart the day of the resurrection and to remember, as in the Easter Vigil, Christ is our light. If you care to add two words, they may be drawn from the Easter Vigil's Exultet: *Lumen Christi,* The Light of Christ.

This vigil is anchored in one central image, drawn from the tradition of the Society of Friends, commonly known as Quakers. One aspect of Quaker spirituality is the custom of "holding someone in the light." The light signifies God's presence, mercy, grace, and love. Since divine light is the focus of the previous vigil as well, the two vigils can be used together, if verbal additions are desired.

Notes
1. Get several votive candles, votive holders, and matches. Make yourself comfortable in *a sitting* position to avoid falling asleep.
2. Turn out the lights or pull the curtains.
3. Light one candle at morning, noon, and evening for each vigil segment, or light several candles and arrange them in a circle before you. This image-prayer can also be done without candles.
4. Family and friends can also use this image prayer as an intercession. Follow the suggestions, but hold the person for whom you pray in the light.

Vigil Plan

Beginning
Offer a brief prayer to dedicate this time for worship and prayer to God.

Image Prayer
Follow these suggestions slowly and deliberately:
• Center yourself for this vigil by watching the candle flames during the time you would, otherwise, allot for

reading. Focus on the flames, light, motion, and patterns.

- As you watch them, think of the light as the presence of Christ, the light of the world; the light that the darkness cannot overcome. (Try to do this for at least five minutes, longer if you feel so inclined.)
- Close your eyes. You may see the reverse image of the flames. Focus there.
- Now "hold" yourself in the light that is Christ's light, the light of the world: this light may enclose you, stream over you, bathe you, or whatever image comes.
- Allow yourself to remain in the light that is God's loving, healing presence with you.
- Remain in this "image-prayer" for five to ten minutes, as you feel is right.
- Transition gently into meditation as waiting on God.

Concluding

When you feel ready, slowly open your eyes. Watch the candles for a few moments.

Offer a prayer of thanksgiving for this time and a closing prayer.

5. A VIGIL OF HOPE

In all illnesses, hope is an important factor in healing. In depression, hope is especially crucial and especially difficult because we are immersed in its opposite, despair. Usually, treatment for depression takes time, but we get through it more easily if we can look ahead, past the current malaise, with hope for recovery.

We may hope with confidence, energy, and action. Often, we hope more cautiously, for fear of expecting too much and being disappointed. Sometimes, almost as soon as it hatches, hope turns to pessimism. Maybe we have been disappointed too often before; maybe, in depression, our hopes need support.

Here is a three-day vigil to support your sense of hope in the midst of depression—hope conveyed through the power of story. The two "readings," derived from the gospels, are found in this book, in Chapter 6. These stories show contrasting aspects and phases of hope. The encounter with Bartimaeus is specific (Mark 10:46-52); the paralytic is generic (somewhat influenced by Mark 2:3-11), drawn from the many paralyzed people who were brought to Jesus. As you reread the brief stories in Chapter 6, you may see yourself in both. In this book, the story of Bartimaeus is headed, "The Blind Beggar Waits Along the Way," and the paralytic's story is under "The Courage to Walk."

Notes
1. For each vigil have this book, a bible, and your journal before you.
2. Allot your time as is best for you.

Vigil Plan
A three-day vigil of hope kept on three consecutive days.

Day One
Morning
- Brief opening prayer, offering this time to God.
- Read the story of Blind Bartimaeus in Chapter 6 (page 133). Then read Mark 10:46-52 and the commentary.
- Use the Questions for Reflection or your own self-guided reflections on the story. You may wish to write in your journal.
- Breath prayer: Select a word or phrase from the story for use throughout the day.
- Conclude with your own prayers.

Evening
- Brief opening prayer, offering this time to God.
- Reread the story of Blind Bartimaeus in Chapter 6.
- Enter the scene imaginatively as Bartimaeus or as an anonymous disciple who brings him to Jesus and then watches with other disciples. You may wish to write in your journal.
- Breath prayer: Select a word or phrase from the story for use throughout the day.
- Conclude with your own prayers.

Day Two
- The same structure as day one, but read the story of the paralytic in Chapter 6 (page 137) and use the commentary and the reflection questions that follow.

Day Three
Morning
- Brief opening prayer, offering this time to God.
- Read and compare both stories, noting levels of hope.
- Use the Questions for Reflection or your own self-guided reflections on the story. You may wish to write in your journal.
- Breath prayer: Select a word or phrase from the story for use throughout the day.
- Conclude with your own prayers.

Evening
- Brief opening prayer, offering this time to God.
- Skim both stories again.
- Reflect on your story and compare it to the one story to which you relate most or to phases of hope in both stories. You may wish to write in your journal at this point.

- If you wish, consider writing your own brief parable about your hope and healing. If you do, you might extend this overall vigil to four days, using reflection and journal time to write.
- Breath prayer: Select a word or phrase from the story for use throughout the day.
- Conclude with your own prayers.

Commentary
Bartimaeus

Bartimaeus is thought to have become a follower of Jesus and a member of the early Christian community. Names are rarely used in the healing stories; when they are used, there is a memory behind the name.

In New Testament times, the common belief was that blindness was a punishment for sin (Exodus 4:11). In addition, as a beggar, Bartimaeus would have been repulsive and scorned. His shouts from the roadside would seem presumptuous, improper. His hope empowered him to defy social convention. It would have been all the more shocking, then, when Jesus undid God's assumed will. Healing the blind was one of the signs of the coming of the messiah and the messianic age.

There is another level to this story. Bartimaeus is "called" and he "follows" Jesus on his way to Jerusalem—and the cross. This new disciple "sees" the true identity of his healer, something that eludes several others. The story, then, is also about discipleship. Bartimaeus has the faith, spirit, and insight of a disciple. He also has the persistence, shown by his repeated calls and by his roadside location on the dangerous Jericho road.

Bartimaeus' hope is strong. To him, the word *hope* meant "to expect, wait, trust, be confident," all of which he models. Paul later elevates hope as a virtue, linked to faith.

Questions for Reflection

1. How does depression "blind" you to the world around you?
2. How do you cry out for help and mercy? In words or in silence, in prayer or in a general attitude of wanting help, being open to help?
3. Do you ever feel the confident expectation of hope in this story?
4. How is that different from excessive, prideful entitlement?
5. Bartimaeus cried out for mercy, not sight, until Jesus asked him what he wanted. What would you cry out for in that situation?
6. Is the active hope of Bartimaeus your "style" of hope? Or not?
7. How do you feel when you are hopeful? How can you increase this?
8. For you, does hope relate to expectation, confidence, or faith?
9. When the wait to be well gets long, would this story help you in any way?

The Paralytic

The lame and paralyzed were also thought to be in a state of punishment by God. However, this paralytic is supported by his four friends who have faith in Jesus; their role is almost intercessory. The friends have faith for the paralytic, who is passive in this story, as are others brought to Jesus. Their passivity may be a function of their condition, but their attitudes can be flexible.

The paralytic in this story is much more cautious than Bartimaeus. The paralytic seems afraid of disappointment, getting his hopes up for nothing, and is portrayed as unsure about his healing. He may not want to take his bed and go home under his own power. At times, he seems comfortable in his state and, in William Sloane Coffin's words, may not have "the courage to be well."

This healing is related to the forgiveness of sins, but the paralysis is not God's punishment. Although Jesus sometimes forgives sins in a healing, many times he does not. "Your faith has made you well," he says, along with other phrases, all of them simple: "Be opened," "Arise," "Be cleansed," and others.

Even without forgiving sins, healing the lame was another sign of the messiah and the messianic age, when the lame would walk, the blind would see, and creation would be restored to God's original plan, including joy.

Questions for Reflection
1. Can you be sympathetic to the paralytic's reluctance and hesitation?
2. Do you find his attitude compatible with yours? Does his attitude seem natural?
3. Does his caution make him seem too passive for you? Does he make you impatient?
4. Do you think hope stimulates the courage to be well? Do you think hope is the key? Or courage? Or both? Can hope come over time or all at once—or both?
5. What kindles the paralytic's desire to get up and walk, run, move about? What kindles your desire to hope? To move, to get better?
6. Can you have patience with yourself when you hesitate?
7. If you were one of the paralytic's friends in this story, what would you ask of Jesus?
8. If you were bringing a friend to Jesus, for what would you hope and pray?
9. Have you ever simply prayed for the presence of God to be with someone or a situation—or with you? How would that feel to you: pray to God for God?

6. VIGIL FOR A TIME OF SETBACK

They happen frequently, or occasionally, now and then, just often enough to keep us from forgetting them: setbacks in depression. Even with the best treatment, the best therapies, there are slides backward. This happens more frequently without treatment. Setbacks are discouraging. We may have to start over in some ways. The worst part of a setback, for me, is the fear that this time, it won't end. This time, the doctors will empty their bag of tricks. This time, I will not be able get out of bed or out of the cave—ever again.

Elijah, the great prophet, had a cave he could not leave for some time (see page 107). He went from the apex of a glorious vocation into an incapacitating suicidal depression and withdrawal to that cave.

Martha and Mary of Bethany had a different kind of setback. Their beloved brother fell gravely ill. Jesus did not get there before Lazarus died. The gospels imply that the delay was part of God's design, part of a new revelation to many. Still, the sisters grieved their brother for four days without Jesus. Perhaps they felt deserted, even rejected. This was a double setback for the sisters. Their close friend was absent; their brother lay dead in a cave.

Here we have two kinds of setbacks, we have two different situations, and we have two caves from which God calls two people. These situations present several questions for reflection; we will focus here, in vigil, on two important questions: Who calls us from our caves of depression so that we respond? How are setbacks handled in the two biblical passages?

We may respond to the voice of God simply speaking our name, or to God's voice saying, "Be not afraid," or "Peace be with you." We may hear, "Be opened," or "Come forth." As we try to discern God's voice, we can be alert for the simple directives; simple but not always easy. We may remain alert to the presence of peace; God's peace, even amid turmoil; active, freeing, saving peace. Most Christian spiritual writers note that peace is a sign of God's presence always.

Notes

1. Preparation: Find a book with at least one photo of a cave. Place it open in front of you, selecting a different photo for each vigil if possible. Also have your journal, Bible, and this book.
2. This vigil can also be done as a one-day vigil. In this case combine the morning and evening vigils for each day into one prayer time.
3. Allot your time for each section as needed.

Vigil Plan

A two-day vigil.

Day One

Morning
* Brief opening prayer, offering this time to God.
* Read the Elijah story beginning on page 107 of this book.
* Reflect on how Elijah reacts [to what?]. How does he call God? You may wish to write in your journal.
* Breath prayer: "God is with me in every setback."
* Conclude with your own prayers.

Evening
* Brief opening prayer, offering this time to God.
* Review the Elijah story again. Now read the commentary.
* Consider the questions for reflection. You may wish to write in your journal.
* Breath prayer: "God is with me in every setback."

• Conclude with your own prayers.

Day Two
Morning
• Brief opening prayer, offering this time to God.
• Read the Lazarus story in beginning on page 143 of this book.
• Consider the reflection questions. You may wish to write in your journal.
• Breath prayer: "Jesus is with me in setback and suffering."
• Conclude with your own prayers.

Evening
• Brief opening prayer, offering this time to God.
• Read the Lazarus story again.
• Consider the reflection questions. You may wish to write in your journal.
• Breath prayer: "Jesus is with me in setback and suffering."
• Conclude with your own prayers.

Reflection Questions
Day One
1. Imagine yourself in a cave; try to use four of your five senses.
2. Where or what serves as your cave in depression's setbacks? Is it a place or a state of mind or both?
3. How do you tell God about your fear that a setback may not end? What is God's response?
4. Are you angry at God? Can you give your anger a spoken or written voice?
5. How does Elijah's choice of location send a message to God? How do you?

6. Elijah seems to be giving up in dangerous depression —and, at the same time, he also seems to be keeping vigil, waiting on God. Do you find it possible to keep vigil in severe depression? How? How do you balance the feeling of wanting to give up with keeping a vigil?
7. Elijah seems to hold out an expectation that God will come to him. Can you?
8. What is the voice that calls you from the cave? What would it say?
9. Look at the cave picture: reflect on it as a place of retreat.
10. Why was Elijah, the wonder worker, given the subtle revelation of the silent sound?

Day Two

1. The sisters are in grief but maintain faith in Jesus, God incarnate, who is late in arriving. Can you hold grief, hope, faith, and possibly anger all in balance?
2. When Jesus arrives, he sees the tomb and the sisters' tears. He weeps. In him, God participates in our human, emotional pain. Is this consolation for you in depression? If not, what is of comfort to you about God's presence in this situation?
3. What is the voice that calls you from the cave? What would it say?
4. Look at the cave picture: reflect on it as a place of burial.
5. Elijah calls God indirectly; the sisters call directly. Does it matter, do you think?
6. Why do you think humble Lazarus received the most spectacular sign of Jesus to date?
7. When you call on God, do you expect a big moment, a dramatic answer? A subtle answer? No answer at all? Do you find that answers to prayer come through other people?

8. How else do you find God moving in your life?
9. These two setback stories both involve calling people forth from caves. As you wait in your cave of depression and setback, can you imagine yourself emerging?
10. Think about how you might celebrate emerging from the cave.

7. A VIGIL WITH THE PRAYER OF ST. FRANCIS

Familiar and well-loved, the prayer of St. Francis anchors this vigil.

Notes
1. There are other versions of this prayer. Use whatever version you prefer.
2. This vigil can be used by any person during any phase of depression, and in times of health as well. It can be especially helpful for caregivers, family, and friends of a depressed person. It is adaptable for limited time, during travel, or when away from home.
3. Read the prayer through once to get an overview, then continue with Day One.

The Prayer of St. Francis
Lord, make me an instrument of your peace.
Where there is hatred, let me bring love;
Where there is injury, let me bring pardon;
Where there is error, let me bring truth;
Where there is doubt, let me bring faith;
Where there is despair, let me bring hope;
Where there is darkness, let me bring light; and
Where there is sadness, let me bring joy.

O Divine Master,
Grant that I may not so much seek to be consoled as
    to console;
To be understood as to understand;
To be loved as to love;
For it is in giving that we receive;
It is in pardoning that we are pardoned;
And it is in dying to ourselves that we are born to
eternal life. Amen.

Vigil Plan
A seven-day vigil kept on consecutive days.

Day One *Morning*
- Brief opening prayer, offering this time to God.
- Pray these words as you quietly wait on God:

Lord, make me an instrument of your peace.
Where there is hatred, let me bring love.
    Dear Jesus, depression sometimes makes me hate
myself. There are times when I even hate life, your
gift. I hate the depression, too. Help me to let go of my
hatreds and let your love flow through me, washing
the hatred away.
- Bring your prayer time to a close with an expression
of personal prayer or perhaps with a prayer you know
by heart.

Evening
- Brief opening prayer, offering this time to God.
- Pray again the first two lines from Morning Prayer as
you quietly wait on God. Then add your own personal
expression of prayer to gather together the experience
of this day. Consider speaking your prayer aloud, or
writing it in your journal.

• Conclude with the last stanza of the prayer of St. Francis:

O Divine Master,
Grant that I may not so much seek to be consoled as
   to console;
To be understood as to understand;
To be loved as to love;
For it is in giving that we receive;
It is in pardoning that we are pardoned;
And it is in dying to ourselves that we are born to
eternal life. Amen.

Day Two
Morning
• Brief opening prayer, offering this time to God.
• Pray these words as you quietly wait on God:

Lord, make me an instrument of your peace.
Where there is injury, let me bring pardon.
   Dear God, please forgive any injury I have caused,
especially due to my depression. Help me to forgive
people who are impatient and frustrated with my
illness—myself included. Please heal me and help me
bring your healing to others. Help those who do not
understand and those who are frustrated with my
situation. Amen.
• Bring your prayer time to a close with an expression
of personal prayer or perhaps with a prayer you know
by heart.

Evening
• Brief opening prayer, offering this time to God.
• Pray again the first two lines from Morning Prayer as
you quietly wait on God. Then add your own personal

expression of prayer to gather together the experience of this day. Consider speaking your prayer aloud, or writing it in your journal.

- Conclude with the last stanza of the prayer of St. Francis.

Day Three
Morning
- Brief opening prayer, offering this time to God.
- Pray these words as you quietly wait on God:

Lord, make me an instrument of your peace.
Where there is error, let me bring truth.

Dear Jesus, help me when people misunderstand my illness, see it as my fault or my will. Help me to explain gently, patiently. Help me when I, too, blame myself. Bring me back to your truth and stop my self-hatred. Help me to help others understand. Amen.

- Bring your prayer time to a close with an expression of personal prayer or perhaps with a prayer you know by heart.

Evening
- Brief opening prayer, offering this time to God.
- Pray again the first two lines from Morning Prayer as you quietly wait on God. Then add your own personal expression of prayer to gather together the experience of this day. Consider speaking your prayer aloud, or writing it in your journal.
- Conclude with the last stanza of the prayer of St. Francis.

Day Four
Morning
- Brief opening prayer, offering this time to God.

- Pray these words as you quietly wait on God:

  Lord, make me an instrument of your peace.
  Where there is doubt, let me bring faith.

  My God, my God, sometimes I feel forsaken in this
  depression, and I doubt your care. I believe; help my
  unbelief. Jesus cries out with me from his cross. Help
  me to hear and trust your healing love. May I, in turn,
  help restore someone else in depression. Amen.
- Bring your prayer time to a close with an expression
  of personal prayer or perhaps with a prayer you know
  by heart.

Evening
- Brief opening prayer, offering this time to God.
- Pray again the first two lines from Morning Prayer as
  you quietly wait on God. Then add your own personal
  expression of prayer to gather together the experience
  of this day. Consider speaking your prayer aloud, or
  writing it in your journal.
- Conclude with the last stanza of the prayer of St.
  Francis.

Day Five
Morning
- Brief opening prayer, offering this time to God.
- Pray these words as you quietly wait on God:

  Lord, make me an instrument of your peace.
  Where there is despair, let me bring hope.

  Oh Jesus, you know the depths of my despair; you
  suffer it with me. You took on our human brokenness;
  you understand. I offer my despair to you and ask you
  to transform it. Hold on to me; don't let me go. Help
  me to give light to others, even now. Amen.

- Bring your prayer time to a close with an expression of personal prayer or perhaps with a prayer you know by heart.

Evening
- Brief opening prayer, offering this time to God.
- Pray again the first two lines from Morning Prayer as you quietly wait on God. Then add your own personal expression of prayer to gather together the experience of this day. Consider speaking your prayer aloud, or writing it in your journal.
- Conclude with the last stanza of the prayer of St. Francis.

Day Six
Morning
- Brief opening prayer, offering this time to God.
- Pray these words as you quietly wait on God:

Lord, make me an instrument of your peace.
Where there is darkness, let me bring light.

Lord God, you who made light, please help me to see you in the dark, in depression. Help me to remember that the darkness can never overcome your light. Hold me in your light, dear God, and help me to give light to others, even now. Amen.
- Bring your prayer time to a close with an expression of personal prayer or perhaps with a prayer you know by heart.

Evening
- Brief opening prayer, offering this time to God.
- Pray again the first two lines from Morning Prayer as you quietly wait on God. Then add your own personal expression of prayer to gather together the experience

of this day. Consider speaking your prayer aloud, or
writing it in your journal.
* Conclude with the last stanza of the prayer of St.
Francis.

Day Seven
Morning
* Brief opening prayer, offering this time to God.
* Pray these words as you quietly wait on God:

Lord, make me an instrument of your peace.
Where there is sadness, let me bring joy.
     Abba, my joy seems far from me now. May your joy
fill the empty places in my spirit. I offer you my
sadness. When you will, transform it to joy as you
changed water to wine. I ask that you lead me to bring
others joy, especially others in depression. Amen.
* Bring your prayer time to a close with an expression
of personal prayer or perhaps with a prayer you know
by heart.

Evening
* Brief opening prayer, offering this time to God.
* Pray again the first two lines from Morning Prayer as
you quietly wait on God. Then add your own personal
expression of prayer to gather together the experience
of this day. Consider speaking your prayer aloud, or
writing it in your journal.
* Conclude with the last stanza of the prayer of St.
Francis.

8. A VIGIL OF SUPPORT

We all need this one. Feeling better, good, not bad, not
too bad—we need a sense of support. We need loving

support in all seasons, but the need is greater in depression. This vigil focuses on support. It can also be used as an all-purpose vigil or one for getting through the day. There is a positive cast to this vigil, using one of Isaiah's best-loved texts, reprinted below.

Notes

1. This is a very flexible vigil. The vigil plan for four days follows, with four very brief verses from a biblical reading, one for each day. You will also be directed to read a scene from Chapter 6 of this book. This vigil could also be kept as a two-day vigil, using two verses per day, or could be compressed into a one-day vigil if the entire text is used as one reading. Finally, the vigil could serve for seven days if the text is used for reflection line by line.

2. Each day contains two segments, morning and evening. Allot time as is suitable to you; try to give at least five minutes to each element. The readings from this book can be done in either the morning or the evening if you don't have time to read them twice as suggested.

3. Have a pen and your journal nearby.

4. Read the text through once for an overview, then begin with Day One.

Isaiah 43:1-3

1. I have called you by your name and you are my own.

2. When you pass through deep waters, I am with you. When you pass through rivers, they will not sweep you away;

3. Walk through fire and you will not be scorched, Through flames and they will not burn you,

4. For I am the Lord your God, The holy one of Israel, your deliverer.

Example of rephrased lines, changing the pronouns:
You have called me by my name and I am yours.
When I pass through deep waters, you are with me.
When I pass through rivers, you will not let them sweep
    me away;
Walk through fire and you will not let me be scorched,
Through flames and you will not let them burn me,
For you are the Lord my God,
The Holy One of Israel, my deliverer.

Example of personal responses to each line:
- You keep back the dark; to you I belong.
- If not for you, I might drown in the night sky.
- A black ocean, too deep for me, never for you.
- Must I walk through the fire, too? Can't I have a pass?
- I must. I hold to you and thank you for holding me.
- To you, the Crucified God, I belong, I cleave.
- You call and deliver me; I am yours.

Vigil Plan
A four-day vigil kept on consecutive days.

Day One
Morning
- Brief opening prayer, offering this time to God.
- Read verse one, as marked on the text. Also read the section on Mary Magdalene at the empty tomb, Chapter 160.
- Use the Questions for Reflection or your own self-guided reflections on the story. You may wish to write in your journal.

- Breath prayer: "I have called you by your name and you are my own." You may wish to use this as a prayer throughout the day.
- Conclude with your own prayers.

Evening
- Brief opening prayer, offering this time to God.
- Reread verse one and the story of Mary Magdalene.
- Rewrite the first verse of the text, changing it so that you are saying the words to God. For example: *You* have called *me...*
- Read it aloud after writing it out. Emphasize the pronouns and read it very slowly and see if that makes the text more personal for you. Then return to the text as is. Now write a one-line response to the biblical verse (you may wish to consult the samples).
- Breath prayer: "I have called you by your name and you are my own."
- Conclude with your own prayers.

Day Two
Morning
- Brief opening prayer, offering this time to God.
- Read verse two, as marked on the text. Also read the section on Jesus' return to Nazareth, page 130.
- Use the Questions for Reflection or your own self-guided reflections on the story. You may wish to write in your journal.
- Breath prayer: "I have called you by your name and you are my own." You may wish to use this as a prayer throughout the day.
- Conclude with your own prayers.

Evening
- Brief opening prayer, offering this time to God.

- Reread verse two and the story of Jesus' return to Nazareth.
- Rewrite the second verse of the text, changing it so that you are saying the words to God as you did yesterday. Then write a one-line response to the biblical verse (you may wish to consult the samples).
- Breath prayer: "I have called you by your name and you are my own."
- Conclude with your own prayers.

Day Three
Morning
- Brief opening prayer, offering this time to God.
- Read verse three, as marked on the text. Also read the section on Hagar's story beginning on page 117.
- Use the Questions for Reflection or your own self-guided reflections on the story. You may wish to write in your journal.
- Breath prayer: "I have called you by your name and you are my own." You may wish to use this as a prayer throughout the day.
- Conclude with your own prayers.

Evening
- Brief opening prayer, offering this time to God.
- Reread verse three and the story of Hagar.
- Rewrite the third verse of the text, changing it so that you are saying the words to God. Then write a one-line response to the biblical verse (you may wish to consult the samples).
- Breath prayer: "I have called you by your name and you are my own."
- Conclude with your own prayers.

Day Four
Morning
- Brief opening prayer, offering this time to God.
- Read verse four, as marked on the text. Also read the section on the crucifixion in Chapter 6 (entitled "Choices in Chaos" page *156)*.
- Use the Questions for Reflection or your own self-guided reflections on the story. You may wish to write in your journal.
- Breath prayer: "I have called you by your name and you are my own." You may wish to use this as a prayer throughout the day.
- Conclude with your own prayers.

Evening
- Brief opening prayer, offering this time to God.
- Reread verse four and the story of the crucifixion.
- Rewrite the fourth verse of the text, changing it so that you are saying the words to God. Then write a one-line response to the biblical verse (you may wish to consult the samples).
- Breath prayer: "I have called you by your name and you are my own."
- Conclude with your own prayers.

Commentary
The act of naming, in a biblical context, meant more than it does for us. One's name also refers to one's nature. For example, when God refers to "my holy name," God is speaking of the Godhead's nature. God acts for the sake of "my holy name," or "because it's me," "because that's how I am," as interpreted by Father Benedict Groeschel. God's calling us by name, then, also refers to our nature and its creation.

Reflection Questions

Day One

1. Look at the line in the text. This is the key line in the passage. It sums up the personal relationship between each of us and God. "When God's Word breaks through to us, the Word tells us, 'you don't belong to yourself, you belong to God.' I belong to this Other, with my anxiety and misery. . . and my successes," as the theologian Karl Barth said. How do you feel about this strong sense of belonging to God?

2. Biblical naming was an act of importance. One's name refers to one's nature. When God does something for "my name's sake,"God is saying, "I do it because it's me," or because "That's how I am." Names can also change. The fisherman, Simon, had a name that meant "shifty, sandy," but as he followed Jesus, he was renamed Peter, the rock. Note the effect on Mary Magdalene when she hears her name in the voice of Jesus. (See page 160.) Why, do you think, hearing her name had such an effect on her?

3. By what name does God call you? How would you like to be called?

4. God has many names, e.g., Creator, Redeemer, etc. What names would you give to yourself and to God to denote your relationship? For example, when Israel was flagrantly disobedient, God called it "Not my people," and the Lord was "Not your God." You might be "Trying to Know You."

Day Two

1. First, substitute "depression" for "deep waters" and "rivers" in the text. Read or write it that way. If it is helpful, you might want to use it for daily "breath prayer."

2. The sea, or any body of water, was threatening to biblical people, so much so that this became a symbol of chaos, danger, death. When a psalmist writes of waters about to rise over him, he means devastation. What would be *your* symbol?
3. How do you feel about water? Drowning? What could symbolically drown you (e.g., work, fear, etc.)?
4. What symbolizes your depression? (Doesn't have to be a force of nature.)
5. Notice that God does not promise to keep you out of the waters. God gets in them with you. Would you prefer rescue? Would you prefer to do it all on your own?
6. Turn to "The Brow of the Hill" section in Chapter 6 (page 130). Is the image of mob a symbol of terror and chaos for you, as strongly as water was for the psalmists? Some commentators see Jesus' escape from harm as a miracle; they read it as Jesus stilling the mob just as he later stilled the storm. Most commentators, however, see it the way it is interpreted in the story. What do you think?
7. Now think of how you feel when you are on the edge of depression. When that is your "brow of the hill," what can you do to keep from going over the edge?

Day Three
1. Write out these lines, changing "flame" and "fire" to "depression." Does that help you feel God with you in your illness? Or is this way too personal?
2. Fire, in contrast with water, has usually been seen as a symbol of holy presence, as noted earlier. Both elements sustain life and both have destructive powers. How do you see fire? Does it have positive or negative connotations for you?

3. Does fire symbolize depression for you? Anxiety? If so, how? Does it create the image of a house burning, for example, or candles on an altar?
4. Do you associate fire imagery with holy presence? How so?
5. Turn to Hagar's story, "Runaway in the Wilderness," in Chapter 5 (page 117). She is in the desert, where sun can kill; where daylight will bring burning sands and blinding light.
   The angel of the Lord saves her—and amazes her. God acts in her life, this slave girl, concubine, "nobody." How do you feel about God's action in your life?
6. If God seems far away, can you offer that feeling in your vigil?

Day Four
1. The passage begins with God naming us; it ends with God's self-naming. Both relate identity to relationship with God. This relationship, of course, can be resisted, tolerated, accepted, committed, intermittent—all left up to our free will.
2. What kind of relationship with God is emerging for you out of this vigil? Others?
3. God promises to be with us in peril, but does not promise to take the peril away. What does this suggest about God's way of relating to our depression?
4. God is presented here as our deliverer. As Christians, our deliverer hangs on the cross. Is that image helpful to you in depression? Is the image of the empty tomb? Another image?

9. A VIGIL FOR A TIME OF PAIN

Just make it stop. I can't take it anymore. Where are you?

Someone in acute depression might pray those words, or a long-running depression can move from a numb phase straight into pain. Sometimes, anxiety piles on, making this phase even harder. In a time like this, we need a special vigil. As noted, images are often more helpful than words at such times. A person in depressive anguish might request something like this: "Just give me something simple, visual, a few words. Nothing perky. Nothing to figure out. No psycho-babble. Direct, to the point. Something that says, I get it." Here it is.

Notes
1. This is a one-day vigil with one segment in the morning, one in the evening. Noon is optional. It can be repeated as needed.
2. In preparation have nearby some kind of bookmarks, a coin of any kind, and your journal.
3. You may want to keep this vigil by night with a candle and a crucifix. You may also want to stay with this vigil for another day or two. If not, go on to the next one, also visual and simple, but moving away from pain.

Vigil Plan
*   Brief opening prayer, offering this time to God.
*   Read "Danger in the Garden," beginning on page 148, mark it if for reference.
*   Close your eyes. Place yourself in the garden. You are there with the sleeping disciples, but you are awake. What do you see? Stay with that image as long as you wish.

- Breath prayer: Select one of these prayers from Mark 14:32-36: "My soul is very sorrowful, even to death.... Stay awake with me."
  "Abba, Father, all things are possible to you."
  "Take this cup away from me."
  "Yet not what I will but as you will."
- Now return to the images of Gethsemane again and stay with them for a while. Then pray these words from Matthew 26:38-44:
  "My heart is ready to break with grief."
  "Stay awake with me."
  "My Father, if it is possible, let this cup pass me by."
  "Yet not as I will but as you will."
- Now return to the images of Gethsemane once again and focus on Jesus. Then pray these words:
  "My soul is sorrowful. Stay awake with me."
  "My heart is ready to break. Stay with me."
  "My Father, if it is possible.... Stay with me."
  "Let this cup pass me by.... Stay with me."
  "Yet not as I will but as you will.... Stay with me."
- You may wish to record the images you saw or your feelings during this experience in your journal.
- Conclude with your own prayers.

10. A VIGIL FOR BETTER DAYS

This is another simple, visual vigil that can work on its own or as an addition to the Vigil for a Time of Pain.

Notes

1. This vigil alternates between three simple visualizations and the repetition of two lines of prayer. There is a subtle rhythm to this format, after you do the

initial reading. The lines of prayer may be prayed silently or aloud, whatever feels comfortable.

2. This is a one-day vigil in two segments, morning and evening. Allot the length of your vigil segments as suits you.

3. In preparation, have this book on hand, bookmarks to mark your place, and your journal.

Vigil Plan

Morning

- Brief opening prayer, offering this time to God.
- Read "The Words That Open Our Lives" on pages 160-161. Close your eyes and visualize Mary Magdalene at the empty tomb. Stay with the visualization as long as you wish and gently come out of it when you are ready.
- Breath prayer: Pray this refrain or select another word or phrase from the story. Keep this prayer in your heart throughout the day.
- To you, 0 Lord, I lift up my soul.
- Conclude with your own prayers.

Evening

- Brief opening prayer, offering this time to God.
- In his famous novel *The Power and the Glory,* Graham Greene writes about a priest, sitting in a prison cell, on the eve of his execution in Mexico by a revolutionary government. The priest thinks over his life, and as most of us do at one time or another, he wonders about the meaning of his life. Will he go to God "with empty hands"? At that moment of vulnerability and tears, the priest seems very close to God. When I read this passage I am reminded that only God can fill my empty hands.

- Visualize the priest lifting his empty hands to God. Notice how reception open hands are, when they are offered.
- Breath prayer: Come out of the visualizattion and pray the refrain:
  To you, O Lord, I lift up my soul.
- Conclude with your own prayers.

THE END—AND THE BEGINNING

Thematic vigils, like these, can be tremendously helpful, designed as they are for specific times and situations. There are other times, however, when it is best to have unscripted vigil time, allowing the Spirit to shape the experience. The unique mark of a vigil is the practice of waiting on God. Five minutes of that practice can work in the busiest of days. The basic elements for a vigil that we have employed time and again are:

Offering prayer
Reading, reflection, and journal keeping
Waiting on God
Closing prayer

For reflection, you can choose a focal point from anywhere. It does not have to be a reading. It could be the image of a tree outside your window. If you are keeping vigil for someone else, that person's face or silhouette could be an image for focused reflection. The vigil elements are listed under "Timing" on page 61. They can be reordered as you wish, or you may simply want to go into the silence and see what the Spirit brings.

You have opened your hands and considered the lilies. In so doing, you have considered these vigils and opened your hands to possibility. You begin where you are. Vigils are here to sustain you, support you, and abide with you through your depression.

On certain days, the field of wild flowers will look like a field, just a field, a muddy dun-colored field like all others. On those days, you cannot consider the lilies. They are there, always there, but harder to see on some days. On those days, when depression seems to be winning, when you are too tired, too rushed, too impatient to keep a vigil, that is the time when one is most needed. When you cannot consider the lilies, you can remember them. Do not be anxious.

Remember the lilies. ∎

FIVE

Pathways in the Wilderness: Perspectives on Depression From the Old Testament

Here the world is stripped away, pared down, stark as bone. The and space spreads out in all directions until there are no directions, only space and sand. Seekers venture here to fast and pray. Seers come and scan the stars. Prophets sting the air with revelations. This is the domain of wonders, visions, dreams—and danger. The supernatural is at work. Demons beckon. Wild beasts roam. At night, the dark has yellow eyes.

Spare and stern and shorn of all distractions, this has never been hospitable terrain. It is too splendid, too austere. This place is a force of nature—timeless, tough, occasionally glorious. This is the great biblical wilderness, traditional background for the struggles of the human soul.

It is a desert.

It is a state of mind.

ELIJAH: A PROPHET IN DISTRESS

Now comes Elijah, mighty prophet and wonderworker, creeping into the wilderness, crushed in spirit, praying to die. He has had enough of living. His life is a failure, he thinks. He has done nothing new, nothing original, he believes. There is nothing he has added to God's creation. He is just another wonderworker; the world is full of those. Enough, then.

All he can offer God is his own life.

He is ready.

"Then the man who had stood strong in his God on Carmel tumbled into a spiritual and psychological pit ..." writes Jeff Lucas, author of the book *Elijah.* The "hero of Carmel [is] now a suicidal fugitive," in a depression that does not lift.

Elijah took no food now at all. At Beer-Sheba he left his servant behind. Then, telling no one, he simply walked out of his life. He knew the desert. He knew where to go. "It is enough now, 0 Lord," he prays. "0 Lord, take away my life; for I am no better than my fathers" (1 Kings 19:4).

Depression in the Wilderness

Elijah's state of mind is plain. The signs of his condition are recognizable. Human emotions stay remarkably the same, while terms change. In our terms, then, Elijah has the indicators of a serious depression, suicidal depression, possibly bipolar.

For this man, the change is abrupt and drastic. Until now, he was confident, zealous, bold, a bit of a showman. His self-image, shown in his terse prayer, does not match reality. An honored prophet, he has extraordinary gifts. He predicts drought, calls down the rains, and then, on

Mount Carmel, he calls fire down from heaven to defeat Baal's prophets. Once again, the prophet is a hero, except to the queen, a follower of Baal, who sends a message threatening Elijah's life.

Did this threat set off a reactive depression? Possibly, although he has stood alone before, confronting other enemies. The text notes fear, and toward the end, frustrations. There is nothing, however, that explains the deep ongoing despair. Some commentators call it just that: unexplained. Elijah swings abruptly from a stunning high to a crushing, lasting low, a pattern associated with bipolar depression.

Once so combative at Carmel, now he slinks off alone. Elijah's self-hatred and distorted thinking are typical of serious depression. His prayer for death is not idle, no passing mood. One commentator suggests possible starvation. He has left no word, no clue as to his whereabouts. He retreats into the wilderness alone, going where he cannot be found.

A Wilderness Vigil

For forty days, Elijah fasts in the wilderness, on the same holy mountain where the Lord gave Moses the law. This is sacred ground. Here, Moses was blessed with forty days in the Lord's presence. There is a cave where Moses might have stayed. Elijah retreats into this cave's darkness.

His choice of locale makes a definitive statement. In selecting this mountain, this cave, Elijah is positioning himself in a way that invites God, hopes in God, even unto death. He waits precisely where the divine and human have intersected.

One senses Elijah's wish that God would also come here to him. This pilgrimage, this vigil on the mountain— these are silent prayers, enacted prayers: for days, at first, and then for a week, and then a month. The prophet has given up on himself, leaving his life up to God.

Elijah seems to be keeping vigil. Still depressed, he fasts, he waits on God, and somehow he is sustained. He shows that we can be *depressed and keep vigil.* Second, even more important, *vigils are helpful in depression.* Elijah had little else to keep him going. Nor is it clear that he will be "rescued from despair and starvation."

The Silent Sound

After forty days and nights, the prophet hears God's voice, calling him by name. Elijah is overwhelmed. God opens a dialogue. After weeks of silent prayer, Elijah speaks. He has some complaints, as it happens, and he lays them out, as always, before God.

God answers with signs. Wind screams, earth heaves, fire blazes, but God is not in them. These signs are empty, pointing nowhere, fading out. It is only then that God's presence comes to Elijah. It comes in a new and stunning way: in Hebrew: *qol demama daqqa.* Translators have interpreted the Hebrew in various ways: a whisper, a murmur, and best known, "A still small voice."

"The silent sound," is the translation I prefer. This paradox expresses what our small words can never capture. The Bible refuses to explain the paradox away and lets it be just what it is. It is, for one thing, a new revelation: God is not in the forces of nature, but "in the voice of the spirit given to prophets."

Now the prophet encounters God in a new way: no fireworks, no thunder—only this perfect "silent sound." When Elijah hears it, he is silent, awed by the power of God's revelation. Then Elijah, moved and humbled, covers his face in reverence before God.

God Is With Us in the Wilderness
What does all this mean for us?
How does Elijah's story speak to us?

I was drawn to this passage by Elijah's depression. The symptoms are so clear and so alarming. The biblical view of emotional illness here is straightforward and nonjudgmental, as we see in regard to King Saul's madness or Jeremiah's depressive demeanor. Elijah's suffering is shown in his actions and in his concise, revealing prayer. We may not connect with mighty prophets working wonders, but we can connect with Elijah's suffering and depression.

His story reminds us that we are all connected through our suffering. This spiritual communion transcends our differences, our barriers of time and space. It also reminds us that depression does not discriminate. We are not exempt from pain because we are good or gifted, or even a holy prophet and servant of God.

Up on that mountain, Elijah does not feel gifted or good, but he never blames God. In the play *Agnes of God,* a saint is defined as one who is "attached to God." This is true for Elijah who knows, even now, to whom he belongs. Here, we find no cursing psalms, no anger. Elijah seems more in tune with the psalmists of lament. In his brief, rich prayer, you can almost hear the cry of lamentation: "0 Lord, take away my life." Even printed, it *looks* like lament. "Enough, 0 Lord . . . enough."

Still in severe depression, Elijah turns to God, not away. Without shame or excuses, Elijah gives God his death-wish and depression, his problems and frustrations, the whole package.

This is a man of mature faith, steady and strong. He has offered up his prayer. Now comes time to "wait on God," to be still and silent, to keep vigil. Just as important, it is a time to wait *in hope,* not fear, and to be open to God's surprises, guidance, and grace.

"In the prayer of hope, there are no guarantees asked, no conditions posed," writes Henri Nouwen. It would be hard to keep a vigil without hope. Most of us would give up fairly early if waiting on God were not waiting with hope. "When you pray with hope," Father Nouwen goes on, "you turn yourself toward God, trusting fully that God is faithful and makes all promises real."

Refreshing the Spirit

At last, there is deliverance—and the silent sound. It is a stunning paradox, revelation, and gift. Its meaning is clear, coming to us through Elijah, the prophet who worked wonders. I think we all long for wonders and signs. Often we stop there, thinking of these as the highest form of revelation.

Called to Broader Awareness

Now, however, through this prophet, God calls us to a broader awareness of holy presence. This is the presence we find in silence and subtlety, not limited to dramatic signs and wonders. Prophets receive revelations for God's people; here, Elijah stands for us. Here, perhaps, God gently guides us, through his prophet, and away from dependence on show-stopping signs.

There is an interesting nuance to this scene. As noted, after Elijah's brief spoken prayer, Elijah's prayers were silent. As we saw, situated on the holy mountain, he sends God a silent cry for help, for holy presence.

It is silent prayer. Its answer is "the silent sound."

God is more attuned to our needs than we are, and God meets us as we are, where we are. Elijah was lost, in silence, and found, in silence.

The story in 1 Kings ends with hope and practical guidance. God gives directions for a new mission and Elijah looks ahead once more; this time, he is no longer afraid. There is no evidence of continuing depression. We are left with a clear message that God is with us in our struggles. God hears the cry, sees the cave, feels the pain with us. God does not abandon us in the wilderness, around us and within.

This whole story challenges me. How often have I missed "the silent sound" because I was listening for thunder. How easy it is, in prayer, to tell God how to help. Yet, with all of our presumption and panic and weaknesses, the holy one meets us wherever we cry out, even in silence.

Throughout life, we find ourselves in the wilderness: it can be a desert or a state of mind. Elijah was in his wilderness long before he climbed the holy mountain, long before he started keeping vigil. His wilderness, at first, was within, a state of depression where one can get lost. Then, walking through the desert, his inner state was reflected by his very specific choice of location.

What Is Your Wilderness?

"Wilderness" is a useful image for depression, one that will color almost every scene ahead. As we explore biblical perspectives on depressive illness, the desert is always there, in the background if not front and center.

But God is with us in the wilderness and will not abandon us there. Wilderness, wasteland, desert—God is there, whatever image those words bring up. I wish I could present you with a mythic image with a certain minimalist cachet, or perhaps a simple but majestic landing strip for the Greek Furies. Instead, all I can offer is this:

My image is a dark forest, thick with trees and foliage, darker still as night falls. I am a child and I am lost. I am wearing strange clothes: long skirt, an apron, a kerchief over my hair. Apparently, I have been outfitted by the Brothers Grimm. My imagery comes from nothing more profound than fairy tales *(Hansel and Gretel?* Minus Hansel?).

Then I "tell" the child that God is there. Now the darkness starts to drain away like water. The forest starts to thin, the sky grows lighter. The difference is the proverbial "night to day." It all happens with the speed and tactics of a folk tale. The child is different: taller, older. She still must find her way, but she is no longer a waif in the wilderness.

JEREMIAH: A VOICE CRYING IN THE WILDERNESS

"Cursed be the day on which I was born!

"May the day my mother gave me birth never be blessed!

"Cursed be the man who brought the news to my father, saying, 'A child, a son has been born to you" (Jeremiah 20:14-16).

Hear the cry of Jeremiah, the prophet. Hear the wise man, the righteous man, holy and true and tormented. Jeremiah's anguish as well as his greatness is noted by scholars. He struggles with significant and chronic despair—depression, in our terms—and yet this prophet transcends his suffering and allows it to enrich his calling. He is an outstanding model for living with depression, for living *productively* with depression. Jeremiah's life is really lived for others, his people. He accepts his calling and lives it out.

Wise, vehement, often eloquent, Jeremiah is a strong presence. His prophecies are declared with conviction and power; Jeremiah's voice does not reveal his "loneliness and feelings of despair ... the prophetic trust in God mixed with a sense of total aloneness...." The prophet's public voice thunders. His private voice is "one of the most anguished in the Bible," writes biblical scholar Lawrence Boadt.

Prophet of Power and Pain

"Never did I desire this day of despair.. ." Jeremiah groans to God (Jeremiah 17:17). As always, Jeremiah turns to God, brings his tortured soul to his Lord, and lets himself be utterly vulnerable in God's presence: "Heal me, Lord.... Save me.... Do not be my ruin, you my refuge ..." (Jeremiah 17:16).

Heal me. Save me.

*You my refuge....*Simple words, powerful, almost heartbreaking. Almost.

Do not pity this man. Do not think him pathetic. Do not presume him to be a sad case. His prophesy of "a new covenant" is a landmark of Old Testament theology. He helps to guide Israel through devastation, its worst hour. For others, he is strong; his private voice sounds "like someone on the edge of giving up altogether ..." (Boadt).

But Jeremiah does not give up.

This odd, pained loner, never fitting in, never to marry, seems sustained by his calling and God's presence. Jeremiah's life forms a constant vigil: watching, waiting, with extraordinary attentive presence—the man of God who does not listen to hear his voice but the voice of the One to whom he belongs, no matter what happens. God-struck, gifted, and guided, Jeremiah never finds his own state of grace.

In contrast to his vehement warnings, his "Confessions" provide an unusual picture of a public man's private and long-running anguish: "Why is my pain continuous, my wound incurable, refusing to be healed?" He cries out, then turns back to preaching and writing, a genius with words and profound spiritual insight (cf. Jeremiah 12:1-6; 15:10-21).

Jeremiah's imagery is still vivid. God is the potter; we are the clay (Jeremiah 18:2-4). The rest of the passage is a bit darker. Jeremiah watches the potter scrap a flawed pot. This is what God can do to Israel, comes the prophetic message. Jeremiah understands about broken pots. His own sense of brokenness uniquely qualifies him to communicate prophecies of Israel's brokenness to come.

A New Covenant of the Heart

Amid ruin, after the fall of Israel to Babylon, Jeremiah voices his most famous prophecy, still quoted today: There will be a *new* covenant. God's new covenant with Israel will not be written on stone. It will be written on the people's hearts, *always within them* (Jeremiah 31:32-33). A landmark in covenant theology, some call this passage "The gospel before the gospel."

How poignant that a lonely man, without a wife or sweetheart, offers us this image of the heart, the poetic source of love and tenderness. Perhaps Jeremiah's pain makes him all the more sensitive to the power of love.

This prophet of doom leaves us with a message of hope and promise. He never stops serving God or his people, but he himself never leaves depression's terrain. He remains "a voice crying in the wilderness": a voice so great, we hear it still.

WILDERNESS AND DEPRESSION: A SHARED TERRAIN

"Wilderness," as we have seen, is a state of mind and a location. As a location, it has several connotations. The scriptural perspective on the wilderness is a complex one. It is seen as a place of danger: physical and spiritual peril.

The physical dangers are clear: extreme climate and wild animals. Its spiritual dangers are less obvious: a place where evil lurks and demons dwell, tempting and deceiving us.

Wilderness and depression share similar terrain. The danger motif is present in both. Often, depression is accompanied by anxiety, a common "affective disorder." In the biblical desert's roving beasts, there is an apt metaphor for the roving fears and self-hating thoughts that circle us in depression. This is not the only danger. There is another kind, the most extreme. It is Elijah's prayer as he goes alone, without food, into the wilderness: "O Lord, take away my life."

Suicidal feelings should always be taken seriously. If you ever feel suicidal, get help fast. If you are alone, call someone to be with you, or go to a hospital's emergency room. These are danger signs: the triad of feeling helpless, hopeless, and worthless, in isolation, with a suicide plan and the means at hand. Attempted suicide should involve hospitalization.

We have thoughts that sound like demons' whispers. *You can't do it, you don't fool anyone, you don't have what it takes....* Most of us have thoughts like that, now and then, as did Elijah, but he believed the seductive whispers. In depression, the negative thoughts can come continually, and they can bewitch us; they sound strangely believable, on target, hitting us with some fluky power.

Demons of the Desert

From the biblical perspective, Satan and his demons are tricky: they dupe us, they deceive us, they lie. We now know that emotional illness is not demonic, but there are symbolic parallels. In depression, when we are so ambushed by negative thoughts, we see them as accurate.

We believe our distorted views of ourselves, but we are deceived. Elijah shows this in his brief prayer. All the facts point to a successful life, but he sees himself as "no better than my fathers."

In those wilderness times, when the lies seem true, we need to remind ourselves that God is with us, even as we lose our bearings. The demonic voices hiss and confuse us, but God will not leave us alone and lost. The wilderness may be dangerous and demonic—but, as noted, it is also a place where the holy is encountered.

Signs and Wonders

This is the positive aspect to the wilderness: It is honored as a locus of God-sent revelation, typified by the stunning events on Mount Sinai and during Israel's wilderness sojourn. This is a spiritual testing ground and, as noted earlier, the background for the soul's struggles with temptation: a place of confrontation with evil, a proving ground for faith. It deceives—and reveals truth.

Perhaps places of revelation have to be on that edge of danger, right on that line between the visible and invisible worlds. Celtic spirituality calls these "thin places," where only a thin veil is the boundary; the spiritual world is especially close, with its wondrous revelations, and also its demons and peril.

Sometimes, in peril or illness, we draw closer to God. We may realize more deeply how dependent on God we are. As we emerge from depression, we may feel closer than ever to God. We may have the experience of "clinging" to God, as Emilie Griffin suggests in her lovely book of the same name.

There are other thoughts that are not so lovely. Sometimes, during an illness, we draw away from God instead. Anger may surface, rage at the illness itself, at life, at God. Our anger may be frozen, revealing itself as estrangement from God.

Spiritual Choices in Depression

What makes the difference? Can we become aware of spiritual choices in depression, choices that affect how we emerge? Even then, can we choose to cooperate with God's grace or ignore it?

Elijah's story tells us we can cooperate. Jeremiah's story underscores this. The prophets bring us a spiritual approach to depression, illustrated by Elijah's experience in the wilderness cave. These are demands made upon us by the wilderness, within us or around us:

- Stay in relationship with God; do not turn away.
- Keep vigil; watch, wait, pray, and trust in God's love.
- In some way, invite God into your life and situation.

Elijah, as we have seen, met all three demands and we have observed them. Though crushed in spirit, Elijah's relationship with God remains strong. We noted the prophet's invitational spirit, as he kept vigil, waiting on God. Elijah raises "waiting on God" to an art form. His is a long wait. He does not mind. He is waiting on God.

The Desert's Gifts

If we wait on God in the wilderness, and if we remain open to God, expectant, invitational, we may receive certain insights amidst the waiting. There are many, and they vary with the situation, but there is a core pattern, a kind of recurrent series, again threefold, of spiritual discernment. If we are alert, the wilderness experience offers

- renewed spiritual alertness and hope,
- new insights about God's presence with us, and
- a future toward which we move in hope.

I do believe in miracles, but the dramatic ones seem rare. More often, I think, God supports and strengthens us in the wilderness, renewing our spirits and abiding with us. God, Lord of Time, offers us a gift beyond words, a gift that God alone can give: a future.

We have seen these gifts and grace sustain two famous prophets, but what of all the others who were not leaders, prophets, well-known? What of them, the nameless, the "nobodies," the "briefly mentioned"? What of their sufferings?

What of someone like Hagar?

HAGAR: RUNAWAY IN THE WILDERNESS

"Just a slave-girl," she might have described herself: "Nobody." Not a person who is noticed. Not the sort of life in which God intervenes. Just a female slave who, despairing, runs away.

If she goes back now, she might be whipped. If only she had not run away, even when Sarai, her mistress, spoke her ill and slapped her face. Hagar knew why. Sarai was barren. Hagar was given to Sarai's husband, Abram, to make a child, and this was done; he lay with his slave and his wife resents it. Hagar bore this for a time—then she ran.

Now pregnant and frightened, Hagar is lost in this huge wilderness where she has walked for hours. Dragging herself now, she tries to keep walking and walking—she sinks to the ground, too exhausted to rise. She can hear a spring of water nearby, but she is too tired to drink. She is somewhere in the wilderness on the way to Shur. Those are only words; she does not know where she is. The night is huge and unforgiving. The black sky seems to expand as she watches and then she is too afraid to watch, too afraid to sleep or to move. Jackals howl. There is no moon.

Grace in the Wasteland

What a fool she was to run away, Hagar thinks. This is far worse than what she fled. No one knows where she is, no one could rescue her. She is lost and she will die here, and the baby within her will die as well. Hagar crouches there, shivering, weeping. Her face is wet with tears, her head is bowed.

That is when the angel appears.

Hagar has heard no one coming, no sound at all but the wind, but suddenly, she knows she is not alone. Trembling, she forces herself to look up. A pillar of light, streaming light, is there, before her. Terrified, entranced, breathless, Hagar scarcely breathes. She cannot turn her gaze away. From the light come words: her name. "Hagar, Sarai's slave-girl, where have you come from and where are you going?" (Genesis 16:7-14).

She draws a quick breath. This being knows her name, her status, her mistress, and more. God has heard her crying out, God has seen her mistreatment. This being knows about her despair, her homesickness, and maybe even those looks she has given to Sarai. Hagar trembles. God knows her (Genesis 16:11).

Now from the light, more words come: Hagar must go back. She will live and bear a son. Her descendants would be too many to number: a tribe, a people, and she would be its source. A slave girl—chosen to mother a nation. Only God could make such things happen. Awed, moved, grateful, she bows her head and tries to speak. Only a whisper comes; only a few words, though she wants many:

"Have I seen God and still live?"

Hagar looks up . . . but the being is gone.

God Always Gives Freedom

A slave is granted a divine visitation. Elijah the prophet and Hagar the slave are given equivalent spiritual graces. In this story of reversal, we are reminded vividly that God's ways are not the world's.

The Bible frequently presents us with reversal. A boy with a slingshot slays the giant. A band of slaves is led from bondage to freedom. A bush burns for a shepherd with a murder in his past. An abused slave, favored with revelations, becomes the matriarch of a new clan.

The story shows us, once again, that God's bond is with all of us and with "the least" of us. Hagar struggles in her wilderness. We struggle in the wilderness of depression. No struggle with despair is off limits, out of bounds, or too insignificant for God.

Is God Too Busy for Us?

"God is probably too busy for me." I have heard many people say this, and many of us feel this at times. Hagar's story shows that God is not "too busy" for us, whoever we are. God hears Hagar's cries and our cries and will not leave us lost, alone, despairing.

Surely, Hagar despairs; is she depressed? We know little about her. She is miserable enough to run away. Her situation, though not unusual, hardly seems a happy one. When we encounter her, she is in despair. More important, she is in despair when she encounters God.

Hagar and Elijah have some similarities, as unlikely as that seems. Both despair and flee to the wilderness. God intervenes, reversing despair, giving support, renewing strength, and promising a future beyond the wilderness. Both receive powerful revelations from God.

Revelation is a feature of the wilderness, as we have seen. Hagar believes she has "seen God and lived" (Genesis 16:14). In the text, the being is referred to as the angel of the Lord, who is considered by many scholars as "an appearance of God." One commentator writes that the only distinction between the angel of the Lord and God is the distinction between God visible and God invisible. It is agreed, in any case, that God is present.

God Lifts Up the Lost

God's response to Hagar changes her life in subtle ways. God does not "fix" the basic problem. Hagar must go back to her difficult situation. She is not immediately freed from slavery. God first frees her in other ways, with graced support, insight, and hope for the future.

Hagar acts in absolute trust, and so she trusts the promise of life *beyond the wilderness.* She would remember that God came to her—the "lowliest" of persons: a slave, a foreigner, and a woman. Even so, she knows God's presence is with her.

This small story presents two great biblical themes. First, the humble are exalted. The "lowly" are lifted by God's saving action. God, who raises the humble, the lost, the broken, reaches deep into every wilderness, desert, or depression. God knows that we can get lost in depression as we could in an external place.

The second theme is freedom. God frees. Pagan deities enslave. Illness and poverty can enslave as well. God wills our freedom from all forms of bondage, as shown definitively in the story of Exodus.

We know more about the enslaved Israelites than we know of this enslaved Egyptian woman. Hagar's story is spare, with little exposition, and the narrative begins shortly before her visitation. We know of Hagar as a mistreated slave and pregnant concubine, but not much more: how long she has been a slave, how she thinks of God, how long she has wandered in the desert. Hours? Days? Does it matter?

Hagar's Example of Holy Hope

We know this: Like the Israelites in Egypt, Hagar cries out and God hears her. She runs away and God comes to her aid as she weeps in the desert. Reverent and awed, in faith, she obeys and begins moving toward the future God has shown her. In the end, this is the only story that matters.

It is a rarity. History usually ignores the humble, the outcast, and the enslaved. Hagar offers a portrait of pure faith, responsive and spontaneous. She trusts in the One who loves the humble, the outcast, the enslaved, and answers *all* human cries of distress.

We see Hagar later, this time with her young son, Ishmael. Through divine intervention, the aged Sarai has at last had a child, Isaac, who plays with Ishmael. Sarai resents Ishmael as well as Hagar and demands that Abram send them both away forever (Genesis 21:8-19). Once more, Hagar wanders in the desert, this time with her son. Their water runs out and the sun scalds them. They will both die here, without water, and Hagar cannot bear to watch her son perish. If she could quench her son's thirst with her tears, she would. How could this be happening to her all over again? Why does she keep getting lost in the desert?

Once more, God hears Hagar's cries, to her amazement, and God is not angry. God shows great care for this mother and child. Before her, again, there is a pillar streaming with light, brighter than sun, and yet not blinding. The angel of the Lord comes to Hagar and her small son. Knowing her distress, the angel saves Ishmael's life and "opens" Hagar's eyes to an abundant water source. The angel of the Lord repeats God's faithful promise to make her the mother of a "great nation." Only through God's intervention, mother and son survive the desert. Ishmael grows up, marries, and the dynasty begins.

God does not weary of us, no matter how often we find ourselves lost in the desert or in depression. This story reassures us that God is patient with us, as well as faithful. God hears our cries, Hagar is saying, and in unexpected ways, takes on our tears.

HANNAH: A WILDERNESS OF TEARS

"Hannah, why do you weep?"
She shakes her head. He tries again.
"And why do you refuse to eat?"
She looks up, still weeping.
"Why do you grieve?"
More tears.

He knows the answer. She knows the questions. He always feels helpless. She always feels thankless. Her husband Elkanah is so good to her. Some men would not love a barren wife. He does—still she weeps. He has to sire children from a concubine; he does not care for her yet he must have heirs. Hannah's face runs with tears (1 Samuel 1:3-2:11).

Soon they go up to the shrine at Shiloh for the sacrifice. Hannah wipes her eyes again. It is time to leave, but she cannot leave her inner wilderness; it is with her wherever she goes.

Drunk With Prayer and Praise

This wilderness even comes with her to Shiloh: strong and spare and yet maternal, leaning over all who come, gathering them into a wide embrace. Her husband goes off to make sacrifice; she stays to pray in this sacred space, this place she loves.

In the house of the Lord, incense mists the air and gathers overhead, a blue-gray canopy; below, fresh incense drifts like veils around her, drawing her into prayer. Raising her hands to God, Hannah's lips move, though her voice cannot be heard. Eyes closed, face luminous, she is caught up in her prayer.

"Oh Lord of hosts, if you look with pity on the misery of your handmaid, if you give your handmaid a male child, I will give him to you...." Eli, the aging priest, watches Hannah. How she babbles, he thinks, she must be drunk. Indignant now, he looms over her.

"How long will you make a drunken show of yourself?" his old voice rasps like a warped door. "Sober up from your wine."

Hannah opens her eyes. Did he say ... drunk? "I am an unhappy woman," she looks straight at Eli. "I have had no wine or strong drink, I was only pouring out my troubles to the Lord. . . . My prayer is prompted by sorrow and misery." She closes her eyes in prayer once again.

Tears Turned to Joy

Afterward, home again, Hannah does not weep. Her husband is relieved. And in a few weeks he is astonished, proud, pleased—he opens new wine. Hannah, at last, is with child. Hannah prays constantly for the child. All pregnancies are vigils. One evening, as she sits to supper, her water breaks.

The pain of childbirth is nothing to her. She hears her son's first cry. As she holds him, she knows she must give him up when he is weaned. Even so, she can't weep. This is her covenant with the Lord. This is God's work in her life, and in her child's. Hannah calls the baby Samuel, which means "name of God."

The Handmaid's Song

Three years pass swiftly, like three summer days. Now time is up. Samuel must be given, in service, to God at

Shiloh. Outside its doors, there are farewells and blessings. Hannah's husband is worried. The boy is excited, he will do well, but what of Hannah? She will be distraught, sick unto death, and what can he do? She has not yet wept. As Samuel goes off with Eli's kin, Elkanah watches his wife. She only asks to go into the temple.

Now, her husband thinks. Now she will weep. But Hannah, standing straight, lifts up her hands in prayer. "My heart rejoices in the Lord. . . ." Her words sing through the temple. "None so holy as the Lord. . .

Her voice sparkles on the air.

"He brings down and he raises up.

"He lifts the weak from the dust."

Like a prophetess, she lets words of praise flow through her: She stands in a circle of power; no one would dare call her drunk. Finishing her prayer, she says "Amen" and goes out with her husband. Her eyes are lit—and they are dry.

SINGING IN THE WILDERNESS

The Bible presents several miraculous births to barren women, but Hannah's story transcends the genre. As we follow its unusual direction, we note Hannah's progress from depression to joy. Without preaching, this is a story of unique spiritual depth.

It begins with tears. There are common signs of a depression. Hannah cannot eat or stop weeping. "An unhappy woman," she feels "sorrow and misery"(1 Samuel 1:15-16). Her wilderness of depression is literally "a vale of tears" and there seems no way to accept or escape it.

Hannah brings her pain and her whole self to God, as did Elijah. In the Temple, she prays so intensely the priest thinks she is drunk. This was also the misinterpretation at the first Pentecost when it was said of the inspired disciples, "They have had too much new wine" (Acts 2:13).

Hannah's depression dissipates after she gives her situation up to God, and before there are any results, before she conceives her child. Then, when she must give the child up, as promised, we may expect a return of depression. Hannah surprises us. Right after leaving her son, she raises her hymn of praise, often compared to the Virgin Mary's Magnificat. No more depression is evident.

Hannah eventually has more children, but before them, and after leaving her son, how can she feel glad? Her strength is in her relationship with God. She has the spiritual depth to understand that sacrifice, as well as joy, is a part of this bond.

Sacrifice Is Part of Love

Her first fruits are given to God, as customary. It is possible that Hannah hoped and trusted in God for a blessing. However, the gift of a child is costly under any circumstances. She also understands that sacrifice is part of love. Her depression dissipates after she offers her pain to God, before she conceives. Hannah, like Elijah and Hagar, shows us the strength and happiness of life with God, who gives to her and to whom she can offer her greatest gift.

Hannah's story is one of depression and healing. It is also a story of relationship with God. Here again, depression and spirituality intersect in a salvific way. Perhaps the story invites us to give our depression to God in trust, remembering the many ways God works to heal. God offers us the kind of bond Hannah has: a personal bond with God whom she trusts—a steady bond, not fleeting signs and wonders. This is a good model of covenant love, the committed relationship between us and God. Such a relationship provides rich spiritual resources for us. We will need them the next time the wilderness rises before us.

THE DISTRESS OF ISRAEL IN THE DESERT

Dazzling signs surround the Exodus of Israel from Egypt. A bush burns, a river turns to blood, a sea parts. A band of slaves runs through the parted waters to freedom. They are led by pillars of fire and smoke. It is an extraordinary time, a stunning dream-struck ride. It seems as if the miracles will just go on and on . . . and then they stop.

Instead, the wilderness appears.

Coming down from a collective high, the Israelites hit the desert's ground with a jolt. The Exodus fades. Squinting in the desert's glare, the people feel something within them give way, collapse, like a floor caving in (Exodus 15:22-25).

This is not what they expected. This is not the dream.

At night, they dream they are home. Waking, they remember and tremble. In the darkness, jackals howl. Again, the fear comes: *We will die here, we will die.* Throughout its sojourn in the wilderness, Israel suffers, living in regret, distress, and discouragement.

"If only we had died at the Lord's hand in Egypt . . ." they tell Moses. "But you have brought us into this wilderness to let this whole assembly starve to death." Like Elijah, Israel has swung from a great high to a crashing low. Unlike Elijah, the people of God have a hard time meeting the demands of the wilderness.

Israel does not take its suffering to God. Instead, the people turn away. Ironically, while Moses receives the Law on Mount Sinai, the people below are making an idol. In panic and despair, Israel reverts to idolatry again and again.

Yahweh wants more than other gods: faithful relationship with God's people. This is different; this is demanding. This is total loyalty; this is forever, all promised and sealed in a solemn agreement: a covenant. Yahweh is their God, their only God.

This is not as easy as it sounds.

The Challenge of the Desert

It is a challenge to hold on to God in the dark, in the desert. Israel is challenged indeed. It struggles as one. As one, it murmurs discontent, even mutiny and rebellion. It despairs as one, in the biblical tradition of "corporate identity," one entity, but shared misery does not seem to help.

This corporate entity is having an anxiety attack. Feeling desperate, Israel turns again to pagan sacrifice, cults, and idols. A pattern forms. Disobedience, suffering, repentance, return to God—and the cycle starts over again. This pattern lasts far longer than the desert sojourn.

This pattern is also ours, perhaps more often than we like to admit. We may fluctuate in relation to God—loyal when things go well, withdrawn when things don't, or we forget God in good times, running back in bad times. In our wilderness times, we may feel as Israel did, struggling through the desert.

Despite the warnings of the prophets, Israel does not stay faithful. In the promised land, the Canaanite cults beckon and tempt. Even now, it is not too late, the prophets call. *Turn back to God now, or judgment will fall heavy upon you.* No one is listening.

Not until Jerusalem, attacked, lies in ruins.

Devastation and Despair

How solitary lies the city, once full of people.

Once great among nations, now become a widow.
Once queen among provinces, now put to forced labor
(Lamentations 1:1).

Babylon has conquered Israel, as foretold, destroying
the great Temple with Jerusalem, and takes its people
into exile. The unthinkable has happened—and once
again, Israel is lost in a double wilderness: foreign land
around it, despair within.

In the Book of Lamentations, "Daughter Israel"
laments in prose and song, but there is something different this time. Israel, at last, expresses genuine sorrow
and self-blame. A kind of corporate depression, pervasive
and deep, settles over the people in this new strange land,
this new "wilderness." This time, she turns to God forever.
Without false relief from idols, she endures her great
despair. "The Lord was in the right; it was I who rebelled
..." she humbly admits. "For these things, I weep ..."
(Lamentations 1:8, 16).

But it may be too late.

Even so, Israel remains turned toward God. "All this
I take to heart and therefore I will wait patiently.... The
Lord's true love is surely not spent...." This is a vigil,
waiting on God. Israel's fidelity is unshakeable, even in
rejection.

Then, a new prophetic word. "Return, 0 Israel, to the
Lord your God." A previous word to God's people is
remembered: "I will betroth you to myself forever, betroth
you in lawful wedlock, unfailing devotion and love. I will
betroth you to myself to have and to hold, and you shall
know the Lord" (Hosea 2:19-20).

Belonging to God

"When God's Word breaks through to us," writes
theologian Karl Barth, "the Word tells us, 'you don't
belong to yourself, you belong to God.' I belong to this

Other . . . with my anxiety and misery . . . and my successes."

Belonging to God affects the way we experience depression.

"I belong to this Other," as Barth says, "with my anxieties and misery"—and depression, which would certainly be encompassed by those words. The burden is shared. We do not carry it alone. This bond with God offers us a deep source of strength, even the wilderness of depression.

In the context of wilderness, we have looked at certain biblical figures and we noticed a common pattern:

- Each, in despair, turns to God, invites God in.
- Each waits on God, trusts and hopes in God.
- Each prizes relationship with God.

A new theme has emerged for us: Relationship with God in depression.

Where God and Despair Intersect

The intersection of relationship and depression is significant. Depression is changed and often transformed by this relationship, a relationship in the sense of covenant love and commitment: "for better, for worse."

Hannah, Elijah, Hagar, Jeremiah, and Israel all show us this intersection of depression and relationship with God. These biblical people stand at that intersection and illuminate it for us *in the midst of depression.*

This intersection is a place of rediscovering to whom we belong, in the experience of Israel. It is a place of a new covenant, seen through the lives of Jeremiah and Hannah. It is where we hear the silent sound and glimpse future hope, as revealed to Elijah and Hagar. It is where we remember that just as God was present to heal and restore creation and the human family in biblical times, God is present now"

This intersection of depression and covenant relationship with God can be a place of transformation and power and strength if we choose to go there. We may not so choose because, in depression, we often feel drained and worthless. We feel so emotionally impoverished, we think we have nothing to give, nothing to bring to relationship with God.

Elijah felt all he could give was his life. Tears were Hagar's gift, and Hannah, too, first offered tears. Exiled Israel could offer heartfelt lament. Jeremiah spun his pain into gift. Thus these were offered to God: lament, pain, tears—and trust. Wilderness offerings, costly and true, come from our depths. We have our own wilderness gifts to offer.

These offerings meet and form new patterns:

- Hope for redemption is crossed with lament.
- Pain crosses love; love crosses pain.

Now, we will watch these themes unfold in the gospels, developing in many ways and culminating, as pain crosses love, as love crosses pain, in God's greatest design.

■

SIX

Pathways in the Wilderness: Perspectives on Depression From the New Testament Gospels

Seen from afar, the Place of the Skull may trick the eye. The hill, backed by strong sun, appears sleek as onyx. On top, its crosses seem to be pen strokes, inked on the sky. Nothing now spoils this illusion. No executions, no crowds today. Soldiers, unseen, remain on watch. From afar, there is only the sun and the dark curve of earth and crosses on scaffolds above.

Seen from nearby, the real place appears. Sleek lines give way to crude bulk—a rough rise of earth, mostly rock, shaped like a skull and matted with refuse, buzzing with flies. Strong wooden scaffolding, blood-stained and pitted, bakes in the sun. A few Roman soldiers count supplies:

rope, hammers, and spikes, no thinner than a man's middle finger.

This is Golgotha, Place of the Skull, terrain of nightmare and unholy ground. Beyond the walls of holy Jerusalem, this is indeed an outpost of hell. This is a setting for men's final struggles, jeered by the crowds. This is where Jesus of Nazareth died on a cross, and ever since, this is where we return to the cross, at the core of the gospel.

DEPRESSION AND THE CROSS

"There seems absolutely no way to talk about . . . depression without also talking of the cross in the life of Jesus Christ," write Berg and McCartney. On the cross, Jesus suffers in body and mind. Betrayed, denied, denounced, rejected, he is abandoned by most of his followers, and near death, he feels abandoned by God.

The cross awes us and moves us as we see anew how God enters the depths of the human condition. If we are to be his, we are called to take up our own crosses, whatever they are, and carry them. Not only is the cross "planted firmly in the center of the mystery of faith but it is a personal reality for every one of us" (Berg and McCartney).

That reality takes many forms: crosses we may ignore or avoid. But when a cross comes as depression, it forces the choice. In most cases, a depression cannot be avoided for long, and so we take it up and it always leads back to Golgotha: the juncture where love crosses pain and pain crosses love. Again and again, we come here and each time we see something new

Before we stand at the cross and the tomb, we pause and stand back to widen our view. We retrace our steps, and those of Jesus, to see the beginning—a glimpse of the early days, the start of the ministry, when an itinerant preacher and healer walked alone through rural country, far from the city, and in most places his name was unknown.

The Brow of the Hill

At the beginning, from a fair distance, we catch a glimpse of him, now and then, here and there, around Galilee. We see him in glimpses, we hear him in snatches: *The kingdom of God is at hand, here among you and. . . .* People are stopping to listen.

At the beginning, still at a distance, we see him come to a town, to Capernaum, maybe the first real town that he enters. We see him in flashes, we hear him in phrases: *a treasure in a field, a net full of . . .* Crowds have gathered around him, maybe the first crowds, and maybe we glimpse the top of his head, the swirl of his mantle, as he heals the sick until nightfall and past nightfall, and news of him spreads.

Then we see him in Nazareth, where he was raised, and there the pattern breaks.

People surround him: not a crowd, we realize, but a mob.

A mob that is trying to kill him.

There is a blur of men and mantles, men with raised fists and red faces, and we see Jesus, the stillpoint, the one who is silent, striding one pace ahead of the mob. His face is intent, his stride is strong. The men are shouting as they grab his arms, marching him forward; all of them had been Jesus' neighbors, but now they all seem like strangers, merging into one wild thing with one crazed voice.

Now the shouts change: "The hill, the hill, the brow, *push him, push ...*" and Jesus knows what is next. Nazareth, built on a hillside, slopes steeply up toward the hill's brow where the slope stops at a sharp drop; a drop to the death. Straining toward it, still shouting, they push Jesus up the steep grade and they are at the hill's brow.

Winded, gasping from shouting and running, the men halt and for a moment, they seem to weaken. For this moment Jesus has saved his breath. Strong from his carpentry and his long rambles, he wrests himself free and wheels around. Before the men rally, Jesus walks directly into their midst. Losing nerve, the mob parts before him and he walks through it and swiftly away.

The Way Opens Ahead

We see him now as he moves down the road: a bearded man with keen eyes and rough robes, a man, perhaps thirty, with a long stride. The town's whitewashed dwellings have fallen behind him. Ahead, the road ribbons out, leading anywhere, everywhere except here.

Perhaps Jesus pauses and sits for a while by the roadside, getting his bearings again. Perhaps he still hears the mob's shouts, still sees the brow of the hill and the drop. Probably he feels shaken, stung, disappointed. This was to be a great day, his first back home, a special launch for his ministry.

Maybe he goes back in his mind to the morning, the synagogue, where he read from the scriptures, choosing Isaiah's great promise: *The Spirit of the Lord is upon me because he has anointed me; he has sent me to announce good news to the poor. . .* (Isaiah 61:1-2). This, Jesus said, was fulfilled in their hearing.

There was discussion, gracious at first, then increasingly tense, stinging and spiraling out of control. Jesus, on the defensive, implied that his listeners were like their forefathers, who had killed the prophets—that was when the shouting began. That was when they rushed him outside, forcing him up to the brow of the hill for a fatal fall.

Here, on this hill, Golgotha's outline appears in the background. Nazareth's violent rejection of Jesus prefigures another, still to come, in Jerusalem. The brow of this hill is linked with the rocky mound still ahead. They stand like markers, one near the start of Jesus' ministry, one near the end.

But Jesus is still far from that ominous outline. Nazareth's incident swiftly fades. He creates a successful, growing ministry. Disciples join him, his reputation spreads, people respond with awe and joy. In this story, the element of depression does not fall to Jesus. It falls to us—in one stunning line.

Here, on this hill, Golgotha's outline appears in the background. Nazareth's violent rejection of Jesus prefigures another, still to come, in Jerusalem. The brow of this hill is linked with the rocky mound still ahead. They stand like markers, one near the start of Jesus' ministry, one near the end.

But Jesus is still far from that ominous outline. Nazareth's incident swiftly fades. He creates a successful, growing ministry. Disciples join him, his reputation spreads, people respond with awe and joy. In this story, the element of depression does not fall to Jesus. It falls to us—in one stunning line.

Shutting Out Miracles

This line, overshadowed by the story's drama, has been called one of the gospels' boldest statements. It is brief, but its impact is deeply disturbing. It says that in Nazareth Jesus "was not able to perform any miracles ... and he was taken aback by their unbelief" (Mark 6:5-6). But how can this be? We are accustomed to Jesus performing countless miracles of all kinds.

Jesus was not able to perform any miracles there.

These words remind us that *we* have certain powers. Through our free will, we can wall out God and God's grace. We may not realize this power we wield. We can reject God, and, we are warned here, if we reject God, we also reject God's help.

Now who is poised at the brow of the hill?

Who, in this story, is really endangered?

Jesus chooses to break free and leave. Others in town choose to stay as they are, comfortable, self-contained, perhaps complacent. They use their powers to resist miracles. On some level, do they know this? Do we? All of us, at times, resist God and resist miracles. We often stay with what we understand: the world's power. We have the choice to turn either way.

God's Many Channels of Healing

When we face the power of depression, we often turn to the power of science. We turn to the experts' power, their knowledge, skill, and experience. We know God works through them; in their sphere, quiet miracles happen.

God's Many Channels of Healing

When we face the power of depression, we often turn to the power of science. We turn to the experts' power, their knowledge, skill, and experience. We know God works through them; in their sphere, quiet miracles happen.

Even so, we need something more. Our spirits call out for what we can't quite name, and so we join the crowds around Jesus where we stretch and lean, trying to a catch a glimpse or a word, not sure why this should matter so much.

If our spirits remain fearful and wounded, we are not yet whole; spiritual healing is needed as well. We long for "this power of God's love to heal, to give peace and, at last, something like real life," writes Frederick Buechner in *The Magnificent Defeat.*

The Voice Sounds Familiar

We stay in the crowd around Jesus, pressing closer. Though we still cannot see the healer, now, at last, we hear his voice. It is not thunderous, it is not soft: a voice that sounds vaguely familiar, but soon we are only caught up in the listening.

He is telling a story as he often does, and in the telling, the story draws us into its landscape; we are in the story with him. He is speaking to all; he is speaking to us. After we leave and walk the road home, we still hear the words and the voice and its cadence. We wonder again where we heard it before.

"These words that God speaks to us in our own lives are the great miracles. They are miracles that it takes faith to see," writes Buechner "... faith in the sense of willingness to wait, to watch, to listen, for the incredible presence of God...."

We hear God's voice so often, the voice is so familiar, we may not always notice it, but we hear it, deep in our spirits, among our thoughts. This is the voice, again and again, calling us back from the brow of the hill. It talks us through danger and down from the slope, leading us back to the limitless road.

THE BLIND BEGGAR WAITS ALONG THE WAY

On the side of the road, the blind beggar waits. Squatting there since dawn, he will stay until the healer passes. People said this one was different, like *no* other; *not like any of them,* everyone said; maybe too important to stop, maybe too busy; maybe ... he might stop. Now, at last, a murmur sweeps the crowd: the healer is coming, the people are shouting, they see him on the road, he is closer . . . closer, there, that's him, there. . . .

A cry bursts from the blind man. He calls out to the healer once, twice, then again. The blind man, Bartimaeus, is startled by his own voice, his words were unplanned. Yet, again, he is crying out. People try to quiet the beggar, but he is shouting now: "Have mercy on me, have mercy—"

Abruptly, an elbow jabs his ribs. Many voices fly at him: *Go, he called you, go on, hurry. . . .* Bartimaeus springs up; someone takes his arm and leads him out into the road. They halt. The crowd falls silent. His arm is freed. He knows the healer stands before him. The beggar feels the power of this man: the force of him, the heat of him. The healer speaks; it is a question. His voice is somehow familiar, a quiet voice, unhurried, informal, as if they are alone, as if they had known each other for years.

For some moments, Bartimaeus cannot reply. No one has spoken to him this way for so long. Years, many years since a voice made him feel known, recognized, welcome. To his own horror, the blind man's face streams with sudden tears. He drops to his knees and chokes out: "Master, I . . . I want my sight back."

A hand, warm as sun, touches the blind man's head, and then, breaking into his seamless darkness—light. Light everywhere, enough to drench the world, and in the light are trees and faces and the road's dust, beautiful, dust-like powdered gold, and Bartimaeus tosses a joyous handful of it, shimmering, into the brilliant blue air.

A Time of Hosannas

Here we see him again, the roving healer and preacher, Jesus of Nazareth. He has shaken off Nazareth's dust. Disciples follow him now and his fame is still growing. In this moment, we see him standing in the dust of the Jericho road. He bends over a weeping man, and all around them, there is a crowd of admiring people.

They seem to catch his joy; *Hallelujah* they call out, *Hosanna!* Praise be to God. They want to get closer to Jesus, even the ones who are well, who just came to see this healer, who brings them all hope. *Jesus, Jesus,* they sing out, *Hallelujah.* They wave and call as he starts to move on; they call his name till he passes from sight.

This is a graced time. There are many such times in this Galilee ministry. Soon Jesus goes farther afield and is welcomed the same way. They are drawn to him, not just for healing, not just for preaching. They cannot explain it except to say he is not like the "others." The time of ministry is truly begun.

A graced time.

A blessed time.

Why, then, does this make us slightly uneasy?

When the Bridegroom Is With You

Once more, hindsight is unavoidable. This scene looks a bit too much like Jesus' triumphant entry into Jerusalem for the last time. The admiring crowds, the praise, the hosannas—all of it ending in just a few days, when he leaves the city, jeered by the crowds; when he drags himself out of the city; when alone, he staggers to Golgotha to die.

But now, at the start of the ministry, there is only rejoicing. If asked about sorrow to come, Jesus might say, "How can the guests mourn as long as the bridegroom is with them?" (Matthew 9:15). He would turn back to blind Bartimaeus.

The blind man's cross is very clear. Like the psalmists, it shows us the importance of crying out to God. Like

Elijah, he takes his troubles to God. Also like Elijah, Bartimaeus positions himself in a way that is invitational to God's grace, God's entry into his life.

Call Out When He Comes

Bartimaeus keeps a roadside vigil, waiting, alert, and open to grace and surprise. When it is time, he calls, he shouts, and he keeps on calling, even when people tell him to stop. He is the complete opposite of the people of Nazareth. He is as receptive as they were resistant, and he knows more than we might suppose. When Bartimaeus cries out from the roadside, he calls Jesus by a specific title, "son of David," one of the titles for the Messiah. "Son of David, have mercy on me," he calls (Mark 10:47). Bartimaeus, then, knows that the Messiah will come from David's lineage or house.

Only the Messiah would be addressed as "son of David." What has happened is astonishing: a blind beggar recognizes Jesus' true identity. This lowliest of men, while still blind, is the only one to see the holy one. Around him, the sighted people are blind to this revelation.

What the Blind Man Can See

So, on a spiritual level, the blind see, the sighted are blind, and the signs of the kingdom of God, almost unnoticed, are shown to us by a beggar who knows he needs more than coins in his cup, even more than physical sight. He knows he needs and wants God.

Bartimaeus calls to us. This obscure man springs from the background and calls us to spiritual boldness—to passionate prayer, to openness to grace, to radical faith, to renewed awareness of God's concern for the broken, the "lowly." God wants to give us what Bartimaeus, unashamed, knows he needs: God's peace. "Peace," in

Hebrew, also means freedom and salvation. For this, most of all, Bartimaeus called out to Jesus.

The Power of Darkness

Depression's darkness is, of course, far different from blindness. Physically, there is no comparison, only figurative parallels. In depressive illness, it is inner darkness that holds us fast. In it, we isolate, withdraw, and settle for dimness, tricked by our own brains to think we deserve this. We become blinded to all that once pleased us. Laughing friends seem to move in another sphere just out of sight. We lose our view of the future; we cannot imagine a time when the dark will dissipate. Our view of life itself may turn dark.

We need good medical care for such darkness, in whatever form helps us the most, and, again, we need spiritual healing. Depression can corrode the soul. "There's a lot to be said for *not* caring," one person told me. "Less to lose." This person turned on few lights in a mid-sized house. Medically healed, here was someone who remained spiritually wounded, and more at home in the dark.

Bartimaeus calls us from the darkness. He calls us to receive God's peace; that peace that is also freedom and salvation, the peace that passes understanding, the peace that the world cannot give. That voice from the roadside outshouts the darkness when we feel spiritually weary, weak, and vulnerable. Bartimaeus reminds us to wait on God, call on God, cry to God, with hopeful expectation. When his sight is restored, he does not stop or return to the roadside. He chooses motion. He follows the healer of sight and of spirit, and sees the world all over again, as if it is new

THE COURAGE TO WALK

Flat on his back, the paralytic sees mostly sky. His pallet rocks gently, absurdly, like an outsized cradle. His friends are taking him to yet another healer. He doubts wonder workers. He gave up on them years before. Still, he does not protest; he cannot disappoint these friends, good friends, devoted and loyal.

Would they stand by him if they knew his secret? He often wonders. Six years ago, he did a terrible thing, a grave sin. No one knew; he was not caught. Still, he can never forget. A few weeks afterward, this stiffness came like a frost and remained. He did not blame God, only himself. He reaps what he sowed. Who can tell him, "Enough"?

He puts such thoughts from him now His friends have carried him to a large courtyard. They go off in search of the healer, somewhere in this great crush of people. Some of them stare at the man on the pallet. A child runs back and forth, laughing and crowing. The paralytic turns his face toward a wall. He wants his friends; he wants to go home. Never again, he thinks. No more healers.

Have We Met Before?

Now someone else comes near, he can sense it. Someone remains there, silent and waiting. The paralytic looks up; this must be the healer. This man has a presence, something that feels like a stir in the air. In the healer's eyes, something like pity flickers, then sadness and recognition, it seems. Have they met before? The healer takes the man's hand and speaks quietly: "Take heart—your sins are forgiven."

Dazed, lying still, the paralytic repeats those words as if to taste and take them into himself. This healer knows about him. Somewhere, they met before, and somehow the healer knows the debt has been paid. The paralytic lets out a long breath. This is what he needed; no more.

Watching him, the healer's gaze sharpens.

The paralytic is puzzled. What can be wrong? He can't stand up. He was forgiven but no words of healing were spoken. He cannot walk, then. Nor had he wanted that; he is quite comfortable now as he is. He got what he wanted, forgiveness. The paralytic settles back into his pallet. Soon his friends will come back and carry him home.

The healer is still there, still watching.

The paralytic affects an interest in other faces.

There they stay while we watch from the crowd.

In Depression's Deep Freeze

If we have known depression, we can feel an odd connection with this paralyzed man. Depression, of course, is not physical paralysis in any way. Still, there are symbolic parallels between the two states. Lethargy and immobility are classic features of severe depression. Some people sleep all day. Others stay in and stay still and feel frozen: "kinetic retardation," doctors call it. Thinking slows, the mind feels paralyzed, and like the paralytic, depressed people can become dependent on others. Of course, we wait now to hear at last those welcome words: "Stand up, take your bed, and go home."

Don't we?

Or do we?

Maybe not now. Maybe later. Maybe never.

That pallet of ours can come to feel familiar, safe, undemanding. The Reverend William Sloane Coffin, pastor of New York's Riverside Church, wrote a stunning sermon called "The Courage to Be Well." He takes the paralytic's view, then wonders how he himself would respond. Would he really want to stand up, take his bed, and walk? Dr. Coffin understands the temptation to stay stuck. He fears that he might politely decline Jesus: No thank you, I'm fine as I am right here.

Surprising as it seems, we can become attached and accustomed to long or recurrent illness. This notion, "the courage to be well," can challenge us. Do you ever feel reluctant to take up your bed and walk? Is that bed like a cross, one we do not like to carry? Major illness, chronic illness or trauma, may leave us feeling vulnerable for a long time.

God's Non-Coercive Love

Not all of us heal like Bartimaeus. The gospels tell of another blind man who comes to Jesus for healing. This man has to be healed in two stages. After the first stage, he can see people but "they look like trees walking." After the second stage, all is clear. We often experience healing in stages, at many different paces and rates.

God's healing love does not pressure us. Sometimes, we think that means God does not care or is not there for us. We are puzzled by God's love, perhaps, because it does not go the way of the world. Unearned, unmerited, we cannot make it conform to our rules. It does not force us to rise from the pallet, it does not punish us if we don't move on command. One of my mentors described the love of Jesus as offered love—challenging and invitational.

But never coercive. Jesus waits for the call from the roadside, the bedside—the paralytic, still in the court-yard, still on his pallet, to whom we return. Only a moment has passed, and the scene is unchanged; even the same child runs back and forth, laughing for joy until parents appear.

The paralytic noticed the child before, but that time he had turned away. Now he cannot stop watching. He has forgotten about running free, as a child—that sense of flight when he ran downhill. He had been active, as boy and man, and had delighted in dancing till late in the night. When his life changed, he made himself forget. He made himself forget simple joys, taking a bath or an unaided step. To try again—how can he? One thing he knows: he can't do this alone. He puts his hand out to the healer, who grasps it.

Dancing in the Light

"Stand up, take your bed, and go home," Jesus says quietly (Mark 2:11). The paralytic tastes each word, taking them in as before. Slowly, uncertainly, he curls into a sitting position. He extends one leg, and then the other. Slowly, he stands. Just for a moment, he is dizzy. He has forgotten how standing feels—suddenly, a whole world swings into view.

There is so much he can see now: faces at eye-level, grapes on a vine and bread on a table, the stones of the courtyard under his feet. He half-turns left, then right; he pivots and takes one step and another and one more and wheels around toward the healer. The man's throat aches with gratitude; he cannot speak. He stands in silence a moment, then moves with purpose.

He rolls up his pallet, slinging it down his back. He takes his last shaky step—he is walking. He strides, he sidesteps, he back-steps, he trots, tossing the pallet away as he takes a small leap and another and then starts to dance. People may stare, who cares, he is dancing. He moves until he faces Jesus. A small crowd has gathered, clapping and cheering. The one-time paralytic lifts his feet in some new rhythm, claps his own hands over his head, and goes on dancing for Jesus, dancing the gratitude that has no words.

THIS ONE IS DIFFERENT

They come to him: the colorful, strange, broken, outcast.

Here comes the leper, bandaged, rags flapping.

That one, epileptic, foam on his lips, still flails his arms.

Eager or hesitant, they come to Jesus. They have heard he turns no one away. He talks to them and touches them, even the lepers. He does something else: he looks at them; he looks right into their eyes. After he heals them, they keep glancing back at him, over their shoulders, as they walk away. They all do this, Simon Peter notices.

He understands. The closest to Jesus of the disciples, Peter sometimes still glances back at his teacher, guide, brother-like friend. Jesus is a man like any other, but not like any other. Peter cannot quite define it. No one can. The crowds keep on growing; the people come and look back as they leave. Try getting somebody who can explain it; Simon Peter shakes his head. All they say is, "This one is different." That's all. What does it matter? All that matters to him now, more than he ever could have imagined, is all right here.

A Mosaic of Faces

Here comes a new line of people. Simon Peter looks them over. These are the ones who all look familiar, like neighbors or friends.

They could be his brothers. His sisters. His whole family. They are not strange or striking or slightly exotic. Peter often sees his face in theirs. They, too, seek healing: people who work hard, bake bread, pay taxes, plough fields, hope for better times. They come in great numbers—people with commonplace ills, deafness and palsy, fevered and lame and bleeding, and, sometimes, now, they mingle with the others.

Simon Peter sees a mosaic, brighter and richer than any in those fancy houses. A fisherman, sun-browned and weathered, he sometimes brought a good catch to good patrons. He has seen more than his share of fine places but nothing finer than this here before him. "A good catch," he nods at the people and winks at Jesus who smiles.

"Demoniacs" also came: people possessed by demons, a condition widely recognized in that time and place. Some scholars see demonic possession as psychosis, phrased in biblical terms. Others see these cases as presented. However we see it, this condition is not physical, and Jesus healed it. It can be seen as mental or emotional illness. In the gospels, "demoniacs" present symptoms of psychosis. However a person with "a spirit of depression" came to Jesus, he or she would receive the acceptance, care, and healing that typified Jesus' healing ministry.

A Healer Moved by Pity
"So Jesus went around to all the towns and villages, preaching the good news of the kingdom and curing every kind of ailment and disease, and the sight of the people moved him to pity . . ." (Matthew 9:3536).

The biblical view of "pity" is different from ours. In Hebrew and Greek, "pity" means loving-kindness, compassion, grace, mercy, and salvation. Pity, as *heed* in Hebrew and *eleos* in Greek, are honored as divine attributes; a clue to Jesus' true identity.

Sometimes, these healings bring condemnation. In one case, Jesus is accused of healing by Satan's power, a dangerous charge. Whenever hostility comes out at Jesus, we see an outline of Golgotha, waiting. Rule-breakers land there and Jesus breaks rules. These healings defy an ingrained belief system. They challenge the accepted view of human affliction. Jesus touches the ritually "unclean," the untouchable, and heals conditions seen as God's will. As we have seen, in Jesus, God's will is revealed definitively: healing and wholeness for broken humanity.

The Crushed in Spirit He Saves

If we are in severe depression, however, those words may not reach us. We may believe that God *sends* no afflictions, but we may still believe that God *allows* them. Through the action of Jesus, we see that *God does not allow suffering.* Instead, God enters it with us and shares it, sustaining us through it. The psalmist knew this. "He will send his truth and *his love that never fails"* (Psalm 57:3).

A homeless woman, in and out of shelters, showed me a powerful drawing she did, inspired by Psalm 34. In stark black and white, a weary figure leans forward, struggling to tote heavy bags. We see the figure from the back. It could be any one of us; it could be any one coming to Jesus. Near the figure, these words are lettered: "The Lord is close to the brokenhearted and the crushed in spirit he saves," from Psalm 34:18, a psalm of lament. On my wall, I have a photostat of this drawing. It brings me comfort when other words fail.

An image may be more helpful than words in certain depressive phases. When you are not in severe depression, you might want to make notes of images that are helpful to you. In one depression, I nurtured a potted amaryllis. It was an ugly short stalk when it came. I could not do my usual work at that time, but I could care for this flower; I could watch it grow and bloom. Images can be as simple as needed. A photo of a lake, a cross, a leaf, a favorite picture.

Through small images or a few words, perhaps we can stay near to God, even in severe depressions. As we endure depressive illness, Jesus, "moved with pity," gives us these words: "Blessed are the sorrowful; they shall find consolation."

GIVING A TOUCH OF GOD'S GLORY

A blessing, she hopes, will come of this.

Not rebuke, not reproach.

What she is about to do is ... unusual. She has prayed about it. Now she is sure. Tonight, she will do it. Once more, she looks at the box in the light.

This box has no lid. It is one seamless square, the size of her palm. Pure alabaster, no thicker than skin, its pale surface glows as if lit from within. The only one way to open this box is to break it. In it is spikenard, the costliest of aromatic oils. Its fragrance is not of this world; so lovely, so haunting, its own purveyor could not describe it. This is her thank offering, worth ten years' savings. She wants to give what only exists for God's glory. Something not useful, except to the spirit. Something to recall if hard times lie ahead.

Another Last Supper

Tonight, on his way to Jerusalem, Jesus is their guest at supper. Their house in Bethany seems to be a haven for him. So they hope. He feels like family, joining their small one: Mary and her sister Martha, her brother Lazarus. Now, at the table, sitting at ease, Jesus looks at each face, each spoon and wall as if to remember them, almost as if he won't see them again. No one says this; it hangs in the air.

Someone hangs about. Jesus' followers are outside, having their own meal together, but this one, Judas, they call him, he lingers—listening? Why does she think that? Mary turns back to the table and her sister sets supper before them. Lazarus eats little, talking to Jesus: *Passover week, it's a risk. . .* he says twice. Mary, holding the box on her lap, hopes that her brother will not talk of spies watching Jesus, or rumored plots against his life. To change the subject, she asks Jesus for a story, the one about the wedding feast. Under the table, her hands tremble.

Nothing could happen to Jesus.

Of all people. Of course. Not to Jesus.

The House Filled With Fragrance

When supper ends, Mary stands before him and holds out the box. In the lamplight, the alabaster shimmers, pale as flesh. Swiftly, she pierces it with a knife. They all wince, reflexively. But then the oil starts to flow—the house is filled with its fragrance. Slowly and solemnly, Mary fills her hands with oil and, kneeling before him, anoints Jesus' feet. It is an indefinable moment: holy and earthy, time out of time. Mary had anointed her brother's body with spikenard—a little, a plain vial, she does not want to think of that now. Instead, she looks up at Jesus. She sees he's moved. No one can speak.

"Waste." Abruptly, a voice shatters the moment. Judas, still there, in the doorway, his eyes on Mary: "The expense, a waste," he keeps saying. "The poor need that money—"

"Let her alone." Jesus' voice has an edge. "It is a fine thing she has done for me. The poor are among you always, but you will not always have me. She has done what lay in her power. She is anointing my body beforehand for burial" (John 12:7).

Mary stands, eyes wet. Judas slams out.

"It seemed right," Mary says after a while.

"After what you did for me, for us...." Lazarus trails off. *What Jesus did.*

So they refer to this unreal reality.

CALLING LIFE FROM A TOMB

What Jesus did, weeks before, was a sign—a spectacular sign, revealing God's presence in him and giving glory to God in a new way. To Mary and Martha, the sign was not about revelation. For some time, they had known who Jesus was. This was about their adored, only brother, Lazarus, who had sickened and died, buried four days when Jesus arrived. He wept with the sisters by Lazarus' tomb, while they begged his help; while a crowd stared.

Standing back, they watched three men unseal the tomb. When the men were gone, Jesus prayed at the cave-tomb of Lazarus. Facing it, Jesus stood straight as a warrior, poised for battle. His voice, when he spoke, was searing, fierce, strong:

"Lazarus, come forth."

The tomb was still. A pale blur appeared. Then, from the cave, a shrouded figure emerged, stark white against the dark rocks behind it, almost a nightmare figure at first. From the crowd, there were screams, then hosannas; people leapt up and fell to their knees. Mary twined her fingers with Martha and lifted their joined hands to God.

"Loose him, let him go," Jesus commanded two men, but Mary came forward. She would tend to her brother herself. Strip by strip of white linen, scented with spikenard, unwound in her fingers, and then, there was Lazarus, puzzled, smiling . . . and hungry for dinner.

Knots of people gathered in prayer, even as spies darted off to Jerusalem. Golgotha's presence was closer now, its scaffold empty, blood on its ground, but nearby in Bethany, there was joy; there was awe. People felt dazzled, as if they had looked too long at the sun, and two giddy sisters cooked. Their only brother and their dearest friend waited for supper.

Now, weeks later, in Bethany, another supper is over. The four of them linger at table. The scent of spikenard still fills the air. Evening has deepened; the lamps are lit. Mary thinks of those strange words Jesus spoke: *She is anointing my body for burial.* She dares not ask what he meant. Instead, she takes out the shattered alabaster flask. On the table, she lays out the fragments where they can glow, luminous, in the light from the lamp.

The Grace of a Broken Vessel

The story of Jesus' anointing appears in all four gospels. I have used John's version primarily, where the woman is Mary of Bethany, often mistaken for Mary Magdalene or an anonymous prostitute.

Jesus sees Mary's act projected ahead, into the future, preparing his body for burial. With God, time does not seem to have any limits. Mary participates in the Passion of Christ before it happens; her anointing the feet, not customary, anticipates Maundy Thursday. She kneels in a servant's position. She performs an act of pure love. She is living out Jesus' mandate, *yet to be made,* at the Last Supper: "Love one another." Unconsciously, she models discipleship.

Mary of Bethany also models a way of dealing with depression. This could be the last time with Jesus. They all know there is great danger ahead. Instead of denying this, she addresses it, though not directly, with words. She sets this time apart as special and sets the sorrow into a context of ritual and enacted prayer. Her feelings are focused into a simple but meaningful action. This is something that we can do in depression: focus our feelings into simple actions; sometimes we can't pray in words.

A simple action could mean brief reading and writing, a walk, a lit candle, or an act of service, perhaps for your spouse or a friend—an act that is feasible in depression. You might try one of the vigils in Chapter 4 of this book, or you might find a small gift to give someone. I remember a homeless woman who came to church for a while. As I came to know her a little, she handed me a business envelope on which she had written: "Ten Fall Leaves." There were ten lovely shapes in the envelope, which I still keep long after the leaves themselves have crumbled.

Some ancient vigils are used as times of preparation for a coming event. Intuitively, Mary prepares for coming depression in this scene: hers and her family's, after Jesus' death. She knows there is danger in Jerusalem but not what kind. Still, she knows the right time to show Jesus her family's love. Sometimes, we can act to anticipate and prepare for coming pain.

Can We Prepare for a Depression?

As a child, I was keenly alert to my father's moods. I knew when he began "feeling under the weather," as he called his depressive episodes. He would stop taking pleasure in food, especially the gourmet treats his patients gave him, items he would never buy for himself. Then came a brooding silence, almost tangible. Between silences, there would be restless pacing: the start of agitated depression, which alternated with his other forms of illness. He ignored these signs. With his brilliant mind, great gifts, and will, he could override his episodes in his professional life. At home, where depression caught up, he was a man somewhere near hell: his private version of Golgotha.

It is very helpful to be aware of your own warning signs of depression, or those of a loved one. You might want to list them and check with the list in Chapter 2. Make sure you have all your medications, filled prescriptions, and doctors' numbers. Collect books, prayers, pictures, and other items, keeping them in a special place, as Mary did with her flask of oil. Then, when depression comes, you have sources of comfort, if not cure.

A Flask of Spikenard Becomes a Shoebox

I believe there are other ways to prepare for depression. I noticed that my father's depressions were not quite as bad when he took time for a special ritual. From a closet's high shelf, my father would take down a shoebox. In it, he kept every note sent him by his many grateful patients, notes collected and kept over the years.

He would spend hours alone with this box, which only appeared before a depression—and, unfortunately, not every one. I would look in at him from the doorway and retreat quietly. Once, he saw me, inviting me in, showing me this profusion of handwritten notes, even letters—all kinds of writing, all kinds of people, all kinds of paper and cards. They put light in his eyes. They put life in his face. They had uncanny power. Somehow, they projected comfort ahead, into the near future, into the coming depression. I recall my relief when I saw the shoebox come down from the closet shelf. It meant that my father would not go as far under, "under the weather."

What would be your version of that shoebox?

What would it be for a depressed loved one?

What would it be for someone on the verge of depression?

These are important considerations. They can be very helpful for the friends and family of people in depression. Mary of Bethany's example can be helpful too. She inspires me with her sense of occasion, her flair for surprise and generosity, her courage to show love, and her urge to nurture the spirit.

Today, she might choose a gift—under 300 dinarii—that a depressed person would never buy for herself or himself. When a friend of mine was dying of AIDS, we all brought him exotic sorbets: mango, papaya, amaretto. Unable to work, on a fixed income, he would never have bought such "extravagances"—to him they were something like spikenard.

Called From the Cave

Mary's brother, of course, was Lazarus, whom Jesus raised from the dead. As we saw, he was called from a cave used as a tomb. Elijah, the prophet, was also called from a cave; it might have become a tomb if God had not called him out of depression into new life. Jesus was probably born in a cave, used as a stable, and from it he was carried out into life. Now, ahead for him is another cave: empty and waiting, a tomb hewn from rock near the Place of the Skull. Golgotha has come out of the background.

Elijah and Lazarus were not left alone in their caves. God was with them and called them out. Like them, we need God's presence in cavelike darkness of depression. I know those places; the image fits. Those of us who become very still, rooted to a couch, a chair, or bed, the depression seems to surround us there. To me, it feels like a cave-place. For those who take to their beds in dim rooms, the cave's outlines are even clearer.

In moderate and major depressions, we lie down and stay down. Sometimes we feel dead inside, an expression I hear from several depressed people. It feels as if all life has seeped out of us. Sometimes when we're in depression we don't care if we get up again. Some people pray for death or think about suicide. Others sleep through the pain, as noted. We may seem "dead to the world" at this stage, and we may forget that God is with us. The story of Lazarus reminds us of God's saving action, even when we can't help ourselves.

How to Exit a Cave

I used to try to come out of the cave in a single bound, in a single moment. Where did that get me? Back in the cave's recesses, scolding myself for failing, and reluctant to try again. I had set myself up for failure. In that deep cave, we can move forward, little by little, over a period of time. I like keeping vigil because it gives me time in small slices, each day, helping me move to the mouth of the cave. If depression is very severe, however, we may not care if we move forward. What can we do then?

We can *let out our anger at God* or anyone else, *voicing it, writing it out.* In a grand little book, *May I Hate God?*, Pierre Wolff writes that angry prayer indicates relationship with God. Not only does the anger release some of our pain, it says to God, "You are still alive and present in my life, and even through sorrow; I am coming back to you and you are welcoming me." Wolff urges *honesty with God when we suffer,* naming emotions we may consider unacceptable. In naming them, we open our wounds to God's healing.

We can also *lament,* perhaps with the psalms. This is another way to stay close to God as we suffer. As we saw in Chapter 3, the psalms are honest cries of pain. In this way, too, we stay open to God. We remain in conversation, as it were, even if it is anger or lament.

Even so, there are, sometimes, phases of depression when we cannot even converse or express anger. In those times, we can *wait on God, in vigil,* and we can *watch the depression with God,* who is there with us, as long as it takes, in the cave and beyond.

The raising of Lazarus is seen by most scholars as "the ultimate revelation of Christ's mission and purpose during his public ministry." The event is powerful, God's will is clear, but the ultimate revelation of all is ahead. How deeply God enters the human condition is not fully, definitively revealed until Golgotha. There is some preparation for that, as if we see ascending levels of pain.

The next one takes place late in the evening, in a garden, Gethsemane.

DANGER IN THE GARDEN

The only sound is the silky whisper of leaves.

Sleep, for the men bedded here, comes as easily and goes deep.

Peter, still awake, watches Jesus, who stands very still in the moonlit garden. He is looking at one unused bedroll; the bedroll belonging to Judas. They have both noted his absence all evening; he left table early. Aside from these disciples and the women in town, Judas alone knows where to find Jesus.

Gethsemane, in an olive grove, lies protected, serene: a safe place for Jesus and his disciples, just outside the city. A good place to bed down, this Passover night, after a long holiday meal and that last glass of wine. The trees whisper, their leaves silvery, but Peter feels a growing uneasiness. Jesus is distressed; Simon Peter senses why.

Cool and detached, Jesus had predicted betrayal, suffering, and death for the "Son of Man," the Messiah's title Jesus sometimes used. It would all happen here, in Jerusalem. Keep out of it, Peter had suggested; he had received a stinging rebuke. Otherwise, Jesus' calm was uncanny, as if he were talking about someone else. Someone might think Jesus was telling parables, stories of death, riddles of rising again. Maybe all of them, all his followers, secretly chose that interpretation.

Now they are here, just outside the city. Peter's uneasiness grows, but surely, nothing could happen tonight. The city has feasted and now it rests. Peter himself is fighting sleep. Too much food, too much wine, an emotional evening. He closes his eyes. Just for a moment...

Awake and in Anguish

Now only Jesus remains awake. How easily this calm could shatter. Judas is out in the night, still resentful, since their confrontation at Bethany. For a moment, Jesus smells the fragrance of spikenard again. *She is anointing me for my burial....* Jesus' own words come back to him. *She is anointing me.* Abruptly, he is drenched in sweat; his detachment fades. This moment leads into one of the most remarkable scenes of the gospels. Jesus was under severe emotional strain, comparable to nothing else in the gospels, and that once in his life he sought the help of others."

In rising anxiety, Jesus wakes Peter, James, and John. "Anguish and dismay came over him and he said to them, `My soul is very sorrowful, even to death; my heart is ready to break ..." (Mark 14:34-35). Going a short way from them, Jesus throws himself on the ground, prostrate. "Abba, Father," he prays aloud, "all things are possible to you; take this cup away from me. Yet not what I will, but what you will" (Mark 14:3536).

From the biblical perspective, the cup is a traditional symbol of whatever God has to offer us, and here Jesus asks to avoid the cup of suffering (John 18:11; Matthew 20:22). Three times, in Mark's gospel, Jesus goes a short distance and prays. The first time he returns to the disciples, Jesus talks to Simon Peter as if the latter has awakened, but soon, all three are asleep.

Alone now, Jesus is in such anguish that he is sweating blood, a syndrome occurring in extreme stress, when capillaries break, leaking blood into the perspiration. In this agony, Jesus remains without any human support, although an angel is sent to strengthen him, a feature only in Luke's account.

Gethsemane and Depression

For people with depression and anxiety, this scene at Gethsemane has special meaning. Here Jesus shares our experience in an astonishing way: God's Son in anguish, prostrate on the ground, drenched in bloody sweat. Anxiety mingles with despair—and we are called to witness this acute turmoil, which is shared, not concealed.

Some scholars are offended by this explicit vulnerability. For me, and countless others, Jesus' humanity helps us to open to God in times of need, when we seem alone. Jesus, fully divine, fully human, "is like us in everything," even weakness and suffering, except sin (Hebrews 4:15). The scene in the garden is powerful and wrenching. In our own Gethsemanes we feel a special connection with Jesus.

Now, through the whisper of leaves, Jesus can hear the tramp of boots. Through the trees, torches stream on in the dark. Armed men appear, just behind Judas. He smiles. Sleeping men stir. The garden's gate opens.

As Jesus faces his enemies, he is calm.

AN OUTPOST OF HELL

Now comes the Place of the Skull to confront us, in full view.

This is Golgotha: cursed ground for cursed men, the killing ground for thieves, traitors, and slaves. Only these outcasts die here. Here they are put to death slowly, in shame, in scorching sun, stripped nude and splayed out like bats in mid-flight. Crowds are drawn here to jeer, then to stare. The Skull holds their gaze, and once seen, Golgotha always remains in the mind.

This is Golgotha, outpost of hell: swarming with flies and matted with refuse, fruit peels and dung heaps, bread crusts and bones. Blood soaks the ground. Blood stains the scaffold, bracing three crosses for three sturdy men. This is where men struggle until the spikes are driven through their wrists, their feet. This is where men scream like wild beasts and strain like sprinters to breathe. Pain stops the struggling. Screams fade to hoarse whispers. As they grow quiet, the men hear the jeers from the crowd. Gradually the crowds thin. Above, on the crosses, men gasp for each breath. Sun scalds their flesh and parches their mouths. Slowly, like ash, an eerie calm settles over the Skull and the men who hang there. Seen through their eyes, the world simplifies.

There is the burning sky. There is the constant pain. The sky and the pain and the hot restless silence, buzzing with flies.

Golgotha: On the Map, In the Mind

Golgotha, like the wilderness, is a place on the map and a place of the mind. On the map, outside Jerusalem's walls, manned by Romans, it is an execution site for "undesirables." Elevated, in view of a busy road, the Skull could make an example of traitors.

From biblical and historical viewpoints, Golgotha is stigmatized, defiled, and off-limits to righteous people. This is the only site for crucifixions, other than roadsides. Those who die here are disgraced and cursed. One of the cruelest forms of capital punishment, crucifixion causes more than pain: shock, dehydration, and ultimately death by asphyxiation; if the body sags, breathing is impossible.

The Place of the Skull seems to have no positive attributes, except one: the salvific death of Jesus Christ. It is here that we see how deeply God in Christ entered into the human condition. Here is one of the most sacred places of faith. What does it mean for us today, for us who seek a spirituality for depression?

Golgotha presents a nightmare image, the inner landscape of severe depression. As an execution site, shaped like a skull, the place is a strong reminder of death. As we have noted, many depressions focus on thoughts of death or suicidal feelings. Crucifixion and depression, of course, are not the same. Their differences are clear.

High-Intensity Depression

Still, there are certain symbolic parallels. The great theologian Jurgen Moltmann stresses the importance of Jesus' cry of forsakenness from the cross. On the cross, God in Christ fully shares human suffering, and the "crucified God" shares these high-intensity feelings of depressed people in acute phases or major episodes:

total abandonment
total rejection
worthlessness
hopelessness
helplessness
self-hatred
outcast
anguish
shame

This is depression at a different level. It is intense and unremitting. At times, the self-hatred is blistering. At other times, in major or acute depressions, self-destructive features arise. What can we do? We need to know where Golgotha, symbolically, rises for us; where, in our psyches, it can push up through vulnerable places.

Severe forms of depression are not only for hospital patients. Moderate depressions can have intense phases. Acute, reactive depressions quickly reach high intensity, often with suicidal features. The state of mind imaged by Golgotha should not be dismissed; it is a condition that can happen to us.

In Mental Hell

This mindset does not fit with the image of wilderness. There, we feel lost and alone. We are endangered and tempted, but we can move about. Revelation and refuge are possible, as is the chance of finding our way. We might even grow more receptive to God in this desert of the soul, as did Elijah and Hagar.

Not at Golgotha. There, in symbolic form, we are in a kind of hell. We feel worthless, rejected, failed. Why are we here? Maybe we deserve this. Every negative event, regret, mistake, broken relationship, and failure replays for us here. Golgotha was a place of ultimate punishment; its mental counterpart is torture of a different kind, at times unbearable, but we cannot escape.

Golgotha images certain depressions; in them, self-hatred and shame are intense. Suppose you are forced out of your workplace or profession, publicly humiliated, then accused and abandoned by friends and associates. This is what Jesus faces, in addition to physical agony, at Golgotha. He must feel like a failure: his mission shattered, his friends gone, his death a disgrace and a curse. All hope is crushed out; even God seems to forsake him.

Jesus has felt all those emotions, those states of mind we consider here. He has entered the nightmare and lived it through. In depression, in our symbolic Gethsemanes and Golgothas, Jesus is with us. When we find ourselves there, we always find Jesus.

The Crucified God Shares Our Pain

This can make the difference between life and death. A friend of mine, subject to depression, found herself in a new city and at a new job. At the same time, her depression became active. It worsened. She tried to keep going. No one in her office guessed that each night she worked out various suicide plans. A few years later, she told me what kept her alive: her sense of God's presence. She was not entirely alone; her life was not entirely her own; Jesus was with her in this nightmare place, her Golgotha. Now, in continuing medicinal treatment, she is stable and well. A positive ending. What can happen for us?

What if we are too depressed to feel God's presence?
In deep depression, are we able to make choices?
What can we do if we feel overwhelmed?
The answer, in part, lies in three stories.

Vigils in the Darkness
The first one begins in the dark.

Outside the great house, Peter is waiting. He, alone, followed Jesus to this courtyard, to the High Priest's house. Peter has moved numbly, as if wading in deepening water. How can this be happening? How could everyone else run away? James, John, gone. Judas, a snake. Jesus, under arrest, under questioning. Hours before, they were sitting together at table. Peter wants to shout, to roar: How can this be?

Meanwhile, Judas is also abroad in the night, here and there, around Jerusalem. He has been to see the religious elders. They are impatient and curt with him now. Didn't he get what he wanted? They have no time for him; they shake him off. The council is gathering to question Jesus tonight. It is all spinning out of control. Judas knows, all too well, how this can be.

An uneasy night also for Mary Magdalene. She is staying in Jerusalem and hears of trouble, probably from a disciple seeking a hideout. Mary is alarmed. A woman of means, a benefactor of Jesus' mission, she has served it since its Galilee days, but this is the big city, not Galilee. City men threaten Jesus, not farmers at the brow of a hill. Real harm can be done. Here, she knows, this can be.

Three Ways to Weep
    One crisis,
    three followers,
    three witnesses,
    and three different stories that intersect, parallel, and
diverge:
    Peter, Judas, and Mary Magdalene show us distinct
reactions to crisis. They also show us different ways to
handle (in our terms) acute reactive depression—
depression so strong, it could become suicidal. We will see
choices that we, too, can make. We may see ourselves
reflected, first, in Simon Peter. . . .
    Peter's story grows tense. As he waits in the court-
yard, one of the servants, spying the stranger, demands
his identity. Others join her; the situation turns
threatening. While Jesus is questioned inside, Peter is
questioned outside. The two scenes (Mark 14:53-72)
present ironic contrasts. Jesus asserts his identity as the
Son of God; Peter, panicked, denies Jesus, as predicted,
before cock's crow. At that sound, he realizes what he has
done.
    That is where Peter's agony begins. Stricken, he
"weeps bitterly." His despair can only deepen as events
unfold the next day, as news comes of the trial and
crucifixion. Peter has reached his own version of
Golgotha, that place of unbearable depression, with its
twist of anguished self-hatred and shame, but Simon
Peter is portrayed as a warm and expressive man,
humble, loyal, and impetuous. He would not hold back
emotion; he could cry out to God in lament. He has the
humility to turn to God for forgiveness and help. Peter's
acute depression, however, would deepen as events
unfolded. For some time, his inner state of mind is
Golgotha.

Contrasts in Crisis

Judas' betrayal differs greatly from Peter's panicked impromptu denials. Judas is deliberate, proposing a cool deal to the elders: you give me the money, I give you the man (Matthew 26:14-16). This proposal may be rooted in a conflict that surfaced at Bethany. Luke's gospel asserts that Satan "entered" Judas. The motives remain unclear. In any case, Judas plans, proposes, and participates in capturing Jesus.

After his betrayal, however, Judas himself slips into anguish. Early the next morning, he goes to the religious elders he knows. Hearing that Jesus has been condemned, Judas is stricken. He tries to return his payoff, perhaps hoping to reverse the results of his betrayal. "I have sinned," he tells the elders. "I have brought an innocent man to his death" (Matthew 27:35). The elders are dismissive and curt with him now Judas throws down the money and runs off. Now he has entered his version of Golgotha. In our terms, his depression is reactive, acute, and suicidal.

Judas' and Peter's stories run parallel to a point. In very different ways, to different degrees, both men fail Jesus. Afterward, each of them is overwhelmed with regret, shame, and despair. However, these are two very different men, and here, their stories diverge.

What Makes the Difference?

After three years close to Jesus, Peter has deep spiritual resources on which to draw He has heard Jesus preach and pray, accept and forgive troubled people, often outcasts and public sinners. Peter knows how to turn to God, even as his world fragments. He could leave that world and return to Galilee, to his family, but he could also leave another way: suicide. This life he chose is over anyway. Or he could rejoin the disciples and try to continue Jesus' ministry. Jesus charged Peter to strengthen his brothers. It was Jesus who called him, Simon the fisherman, and renamed him Peter, Petrus, the rock. Peter will try to live out what Jesus began.

Judas, meanwhile, makes his decision. He must see himself as unforgivable and irredeemable. There are options for him, however. Judas could leave town and start over. Father Benedict Groeschel suggests another option: Judas, repentant, before the cross. Judas, however, cannot see alternatives, a feature of suicidal thinking. No one knows if he turned to God. We do know that he turns to the religious establishment, which dismisses him. Hopeless, alone, perhaps bitter, Judas goes off and hangs himself from a tree, though he would know this is prohibited by scripture: "Cursed is everyone who hangs from a tree" (Deuteronomy 21:23). Judas' chosen form of death is a suicide note: *Cursed am I, Judas.* Judas hangs himself while Jesus hangs from the cross.

The Steadfast Witness

At the cross, we first see Mary Magdalene, often *wrongly confused with a presumed prostitute in Luke's gospel.* In addition to financial support, Mary serves Jesus' ministry in a domestic role: sewing, cooking, marketing. Her situation and resources suggest a mature woman, expert at running a household. Jesus healed her of "seven demons"; once healed, she served the ministry from Galilee to Jerusalem.

In all four gospels, Mary Magdalene is the one consistent witness to Jesus' crucifixion. Other women come, their names varying. All male disciples are absent, except in John's gospel: John escorts Mary, the mother of Jesus, to the cross, then takes her into his care.

Mary Magdalene is also at the deposition and hasty burial of Jesus, attended by Joseph of Arimathea, who donates his tomb. That night Mary Magdalene and another woman keep vigil there. After the Sabbath, preparing to anoint Jesus' body, she buys aromatic oil.

She weeps, she watches. Again, her ways suggest a mature woman, keeping life on track, even as she weeps. Perhaps she has learned to abide with suffering rather than hurry it, rush it away. Like Peter, she was with Jesus over time. Her spiritual resources would also be special, supporting her through her difficult long vigils.

Three witnesses,

three followers,

one crisis,

and three different stories.

We have watched them intersect, parallel, and diverge. Each response to crisis is distinct from the others. Each figure shows us differing ways to handle and bear acute reactive depression, which can quickly spiral out of control and turn destructive, as we have seen.

Choices in Chaos

But what of us?

Can we make choices in depression?

How can *we* cope with its serious forms?

What if we are too depressed to feel God's presence?

These questions prompt reflection. Generally, therapists advise against life-changing decisions in depression: to marry, move, quit a job, and the like. Other decisions should be postponed if they involve too much disruption or change. Still, there are two fundamental choices we can and must make: *Choosing to live or die. Choosing to be open or closed to God's presence.*

Earlier, in Nazareth, we saw people who chose life without God's presence, intentionally rejecting or resisting it. We also saw the choices of Judas, Peter, and Mary

Magdalene in the midst of crisis and intense depression. Two are positive models. One is a sad cautionary tale.

We choose God, but feel afraid to open up.

What can we do?

We choose openness, but feel too bad to pray.

Now what?

Does the God thing make a difference with depression?

Really and truly?

There are times, I know, when depression is so intense, we cannot sense God's presence. We choose to be open, but feel let down. Other times, no matter how we want God's presence, we feel too fragile, too self-protective, too afraid to open up in any way.

Often, very depressed people just want to curl up in a ball. It is even hard to open our body's shape. This is not the dark night of the soul. That is purely spiritual. This is across-the-board, pervasive depression. In acute, intense depressive episodes, we cannot sense God, we cannot see God. . . but we can see Golgotha.

The place is an image of where we are, emotionally. Then, of all times, when we are most desperate to find a way out, we need to look directly at the place. We look around at the Place of the Skull.

If we can see Golgotha, we can see Jesus.

THE CRUCIFIED GOD

Jurgen Moltmann, the highly esteemed theologian, sees Jesus as "the crucified God." This theology goes back five hundred years. There on the cross, in that concentration of evil and sin, cursed and outcast, affliction and anguish, in Jesus, God's love is fully disclosed in the very last place we expect.

This is where, most radically, God takes on and becomes a curse for us, becomes suffering, becomes sin, takes on evil, affliction—*out of love for us.* The "crucified God" takes up our suffering, even our sense of God-forsakenness, in our worst depressions, which Jesus has felt himself.

"In the cross of Jesus," writes Rev. Tony Kelly, "evil was outwitted by that excess of love on God's part."

Does this really make a difference in depression?

I believe it does.

In my experience, nothing human, nothing except the cross can fully confront depression's hell. Only the crucified God can stand against that and stand with us. Intense depression is far stronger than most of us believe, and it can be extremely destructive.

Sadly enough, there is supporting evidence.

Talented and Tormented

There is a long tragic list of gifted people who have succumbed to that hell—extraordinary spirits who enriched the world's life but, in depression, took their own. There is a disturbingly high correlation between depression and genius and artistic creativity. Most of the great English poets were depressive, as were Charles Dickens, Robert Schumann, Vincent Van Gogh, and Winston Churchill. The names of these people can and do fill books. An alarming number of them took their own lives.

Even with the advanced treatments available now, depression can still wound our spirits and distort our lives. The illness can terrorize us with its threatened return. So easily, it can cause us to live too carefully, so gingerly, so tentatively, we stop tasting and touching life much at all. We restrict our efforts, our plans and hopes, fearing we might rouse depression back into action.

These fears are not baseless. Most depressions, ninety percent, recur. Even if they receive state-of-the-art treatment, depression can and will break through. Such breaks are profoundly discouraging. It is like starting all over again, and this time, we dread, the depression will not leave us.

Most of us could not bear this if not for the crucified God on the cross, bearing this with us—God's power, not ours, strong where we are weak. "My grace is sufficient for you; for when you are weak, I am strong," God tells St. Paul.

In short, when depression blinds us to God, we need to look around at Golgotha, where we are—and there we find Jesus, the crucified God. There we find the cross, where God's love is disclosed; love that is power, standing with us against depression's hells and taking them into himself for us. He knows we cannot. We need to realize that we cannot do this all on our own.

On the cross, Paul says, Jesus became a curse for us, became sin for us. On the cross, "... it was our infirmities that he bore, our sufferings that he endured," as Isaiah foresaw the Suffering Servant to come (Isaiah 53:4-5). On the cross, Jesus faces what we cannot face.

His Death Releases New Life

There is another way that the crucified God's saving action is shown. This is a different aspect of what Jesus did for us on the cross. "I believe that by his dying, he [Jesus] released into the world an entirely new kind of life, his kind of life ... making alive and whole all who will only kneel to drink," Frederick Buechner writes in *The Hungering Dark.*

A seed must die in the ground to give fruit.

A flask must shatter to release its fragrance.

A shell must break to release the fledgling.

The poets and prophets and saints have been telling us this for thousands of years and somehow it just keeps slipping away from us—perhaps the images are too threatening, too costly.

Something must die or shatter or end for serious change to occur. We know this; we have seen this. Something must be surrendered and sacrificed, and this is not comfortable news. Perhaps, like the disciples who abandoned Jesus, we fear proximity to the cross; we might be nailed to the next one ourselves.

And yet, and still, and even so—we want to belong to the crucified God, whose love stands with us in our depressions, whose love has the power to turn hell to hope. Bonhoeffer asserts that it is costlier *not* to be a disciple, and part of us catches the truth in that too.

How Do We Open Our Hands?

Henri Nouwen wrote of a woman clenching a coin. An elderly woman, she was brought into a psychiatric center, where she struggled, wild, swinging out, as the doctors took her things. There was something she held back in her hand, something unseen at first. It was "one small coin she gripped in her fist and would not give up.... It was as though she would lose her very self along with that coin.... She would have nothing more and be nothing more."

That's always the fear, isn't it?

It is painful to catch even a glimpse of ourselves in this story. Do we swing out in panic and grip our coin? We look at our clenched fists and we wince. Maybe depression has taught us to clutch what we've got, but how do we release ourselves into the spacious terrain of God's heart? How can we learn to open our hands?

Not by force, not by threats. The right words must come.

How easily, then, we would open our hands.

The Words That Open Our Lives

Perhaps the right words come here, in a cemetery just outside Jerusalem, as the sky starts to lighten with dawn. Now it is the third day. Jesus is dead. Mary Magdalene and two others go to the tomb where Jesus was laid, to anoint the body.

However, as they approach the tomb, they are startled —there before it, a strange and radiant being appears, so bright there is a resemblance to lightning. Terrified, the women draw back, and then they hear what the angel tells them: *"Be not afraid"* (Matthew 28:5).

Perhaps we can unclench our fists if we hear those simple words, spoken in Nazareth and Bethlehem when the most wondrous events were beginning. *Be not afraid—to* open your hand, to open your self. Be not afraid of the One who rules Golgotha with open arms.

Mary Magdalene hears those words . . . and one more.

Later, she stands alone at the empty tomb. Peter and John have come and gone. No one can understand what has happened. In their frame of reference, they see only two possibilities: Jesus' body was stolen or moved. Now, at the empty tomb, Mary Magdalene weeps. A man, maybe the gardener, asks her why. She explains. "If it is you, sir, who removed him," she offers, "tell me where you have laid him and I will take him away." She wipes her eyes.

And then, transforming everything: one word.

The man speaks her name: *"Mary."*

This is the voice she knows. This is his voice, no other. Looking up, she sees Jesus: alive, real, risen, talking to her, saying her name. "Once again, the intimate and the cosmic conjoin: through the intimacy of Mary's name, the reality of the resurrection is revealed" (Ringe, p. 301).

Mary understands. Death is not the end. Golgotha and the cross are not the final words. The words of Jesus, simple words, small words, softly spoken, go on with the telling of this story.

Be not afraid.

Mary. Tell the others.

This tomb, open-mouthed, gapes in wonder, not pain. It no longer hoards death; it gives life, his life, released to them all. He has spoken of this, the seed that must die to give life. She looks at the tomb and sees a grain of wheat; a flask of spikenard like the one in her hand.

Be not afraid.

Listen. He lives.

He has sent me to tell you. ∎

SEVEN

Unlocking the Door: Selected Guides for a Spirituality of Depression

Peace be with you.
We still listen for those words.
Peace be with you.
We have strained to hear those words, that voice, for centuries, ever since that night when Jesus entered the disciples locked room. Ever since he gave them that greeting, we have hoped to hear it in his voice again. We speak the greeting in church but still long to find it in our own lives. It turns out that is not so east, yet we long for that peace—the peace that fills us with such courage, such joy, we cannot remember why we wanted anything else or why we were afraid.

This peace is pure gift and, in the end, such gifts may never be explicable. In the end, the peace that Jesus offers is himself, his presence, and so, in our own locked rooms, we listen; we wait. The waiting may begin to seem long, too long; unrewarding, even tedious. After a while, we may become discouraged and then, gradually, disconnected. In time, that resurrection evening in Jerusalem becomes remote, lacking impact on our lives today. It was all so long ago. It was far away. So much has changed. So much has happened between now and then.

Will we give up? Let go of the hope? Maybe God's voice was only for those who lived in biblical times. Maybe we're only kidding ourselves. Maybe what we wanted was only a fantasy, an outmoded myth. What if we unlock the door and open it—and no one is there?

Calling All Witnesses

As we wonder and doubt and seek, we remember that "we are surrounded by so great a cloud of witnesses," in St. Paul's words (Hebrews 12:1). Beyond biblical times, a great company of believers has encountered Christ's presence and passed their accounts along. Through two thousand years, this testimony has helped *us* to feel a sense of that presence, vital and compelling as it was when Jesus first said, "Follow me." Down the centuries, all these witnesses have inspired and challenged us to wait, watch, and pray. Now, as we listen to some of these voices, our spiritual senses can open once again. We are being readied for the next step, on our own.

In Our *Town*, Thornton Wilder's classic play, the heroine asks the wise man if anyone "realizes" how precious life is while we live it. How often do we listen, really listen, to one another and to God? Does anyone look, really look, at another and at the glory of God in ordinary life as it is lived? The answer from the wise man is simple:

"The poets and saints, they do; some."

And so, to the poets and saints, we turn. Like music, poetry often catches what is almost inexpressible. Some saints were poets; some poets, saints. They all knew the light of God's presence and passed it on, flame kindling flame. Christ's presence, as we have seen, has often been imaged by light—from the new fire of Easter to the banks of vigil candles dancing in the nave of a cathedral.

Beyond the lit wicks, in many churches, I recall looking up and up at the glow of stained-glass windows, framing figures that almost seemed to breathe, luminous, alive, as shifting light filtered through them. In medieval cathedrals, you can "read" the message or lesson in a window. The stained glass itself is a kind of visual poetry, and, like poems, the windows speak to us in images.

Think of this chapter, then, as a chapel. Its windows are lives, lit by God's presence, offering images to guide us. We come to this chapel as pilgrims, seeking wisdom on the eve of our own spiritual ventures. We seek insight, we seek inspiration, and we ask a blessing.

This small chapel has space for just a few windows, but they are richly cast and flood the chapel with brilliant colors. The windows are paired and each pair illuminates a shared motif. Each window, dedicated to a spiritual guide, may hold a message for you.

In this chapel, you find saints and sinners and some who have been both. There is nothing special or strange about the stuff of which the saints are made. In the play *Agnes of God,* the prioress notes that the saints were sometimes "slightly off-center." Some of them were "a little crazy," she says later, "but all were attached to God." That is what made them saints, she says, flaws and all. In the windows of this chapel, you will find the figures of very human people, all of them "attached to God."

A whole lifetime cannot fit into one window, so we will approach each one for a particular gift. Perhaps, among these figures, you will find the gifts and messages you seek.

+++

Cultivating the Spirit: Thomas Merton and Henri Nouwen

THOMAS MERTON: WALKING WITHOUT KNOWING THE WAY

"My Lord God, I have no idea where I am going. I do not see the road ahead of me. I cannot know for certain where it will end. Nor do I really know myself, and the fact that I think I am following your will does not mean that I am actually doing so. But I believe the desire to please you does in fact please you. And I hope I have that desire in all that I am doing.... And I know that if I do this, you will lead me by the right road though I may know nothing about it. Therefore will I trust you always, though I seem to be lost and in the shadows of death. I will not fear, for you are ever with me and you will never leave me to face my perils alone."

This could be the voice of a pilgrim, a seeker, a disciple—or the voice of someone on the edge of depression. In fact, this is the voice of Thomas Merton, expressing modern angst and uncertainty, along with the serious devotion of the Middle Ages, an unusual combination, but then, so was Merton: unconventional, gifted, original, passionately dedicated to God.

After a hedonistic youth, Merton went through a powerful conversion experience which led to dramatic change in his life. He became a Roman Catholic and a Trappist monk. He also turned into a gifted, popular, and prolific author; his *Seven Storey Mountain is* a spiritual classic. As an advocate of Catholic-Buddhist dialogue, Merton was also sometimes controversial. Above all, he was an extraordinary spiritual writer and guide. His premature death in 1968 was a great loss.

Seeing Spirituality as an Attitude

Merton gets right at our modern spiritual blocks. He warns against anyone promising a magic method, technique, or tricks of the trade. Spiritual practice is an *attitude,* an *outlook,* rather than a method or spiritual gimmickry. A spiritual outlook has continuity—a good fit with the practice and continuity of vigils, grounded in the overall vigil spirit.

An outlook or attitude is consistent. It carries over into all that you do, integrated with your vigil time. Merton sees the spiritual life as an integrated whole, a continuous movement of the spirit that undergirds work, recreation, solitude, and community life. He understands the often-missed meaning of Jesus' parables of persistence: the widow who nags the judge into judgment, the friend at midnight who keeps knocking at his neighbor's door. Jesus urges us to keep asking, knocking, and seeking, but is he saying that we must pester God? Must we become spiritual nags to get God's attention?

Jesus is saying, as Merton knew, that a God-centered attitude is a *continuous movement, attitude, or outlook.* Continuity is also helpful to us in depression, when we need support on which we can rely each day, not one "quick fix." In fact, if we expect a "quick fix," we might grow disappointed, disaffected, and finally resistant to God.

Merton knows all about this. His own spiritual journey was a struggle. He knows how resistance to God can become entrenched. Resistance may come from anger at

God, frozen in place, or from subtler sources, often overlooked: spiritual inertia, tepidness, apathy, coldness, and lack of confidence. These are insidious forms of "passive resistance," half-hidden blocks to which we must be alert. Resistance can become a matter for serious concern. Merton warns that lasting, deliberate, and stubborn resistance to God can be a sign of a soul in spiritual trouble, even danger.

When we are depressed, of course, we feel inert and apathetic because of illness, but these attitudes can become habits. After a depression, we might check to see if it has left behind some baggage we don't want. The post-depression phase can be very important. We may experience "phantom depression"; we may retain coping mechanisms we used during the illness but no longer need. If you feel resistance, you may try to write it in your log—and keep on going.

Discovering God at Work in Your Soul

Merton wants us to move past resistance because he so wants us to know that "God is really and truly present and working there" in our souls. God's image in us, buried by sin, Merton says, rises when God's Spirit is sent into us and "becomes for us the source of a new life, a new identity and a new mode of action." In this we must trust even if we cannot see it at first.

This is tremendously reassuring when we are lost in a struggle with depression and doubt. It is all the more comforting to hear Merton, who was no stranger to any of these, assure us from his own experience. Trust, he knows, cannot be forced, but rather cultivated as an outlook, over time. The vigil practice gives us that time and Thomas Merton gives us the inspiration and the insight.

One of his greatest insights, the idea of "attitude" rather than "method," expands to encompass the spiritual life as a whole; resistance, seen in this context, becomes less powerful. Merton is a guide who beckons us on to see what he sees, to share what he glimpses ahead.

A spiritual outlook does not have to be somber. Merton calls us to discipline and freedom: "Every plant that stands in the light of the sun is a saint and an outlaw. . . . Every blade of grass is an angel singing in a shower of glory. These are worlds unto themselves. . . . The fire of a wild white sun has eaten up the distance between hope and despair," he writes. Speaking to himself: "Dance in the sun, you tepid idiot. Wake up and dance. . . . You fool, the prisons are open."

The prisons are open.

The room is unlocked.

Our spirits can be unsealed.

Finally, Merton wants to *wake us* anew to God's glory, to shake us from inertia and "tepidness"—inviting, summoning, cajoling our spirits to dance in "fields that smell of sunrise." This spiritual "awakeness" comes singing out of this excerpted poem, one of many by Merton himself.

THE TRAPPIST ABBEY: MATINS [excerpt]

When the full fields begin to smell of sunrise
And the valleys sing in their sleep,
The pilgrim moon pours over the solemn darkness
Her waterfalls of silence,
And then departs, up the avenue of trees. . . .
Now kindle in the windows of this ladyhouse, my soul,
Your childish clear awakeness:
Burn in the country night
Your wise and sleepless lamp.

For, from the frowning tower, the windy belfry,
Sudden the bells come, bridegrooms,
And fill the echoing dark with love and fear.
—Thomas Merton

+++

HENRI NOUWEN: SETTING ASIDE YOUR SPIRITUAL SPACE

You have two standing appointments today. Sorry, these can't be rescheduled, can't be changed.

In your office or at home, when you shut the door for your appointment, there may be some curiosity. What kind of appointment takes place in silence? This is no meeting, no business lunch. What is it then? What's going on in there?

This is your time for being with God—something you do not need to explain. "We do not take the spiritual life seriously if we do not set aside some time to be with God and to listen to him," wrote Henri Nouwen, the well-known priest, psychologist, author, and teacher. "We may have to write it down in black and white on our daily calendar so that nobody else will take away this time."

Creating a Spiritual Covenant

As we engage in the process of keeping vigil, Nouwen sets "time with God" into the larger context of the spiritual life. The spiritual life, in turn, demands our commitment "to listen to God, who constantly speaks but whom we seldom hear." This is the way, Nouwen says, we come to realize that God is there with us, "even if we do not yet hear him...."

At such times, you might find a covenant helpful. Throughout the Old Testament, we noticed the importance of a covenant relationship. You can make such a covenant with God in any way that works for you. You might want to draft a contract and keep it in a safe place. You may want a loved one to witness it for you. The covenant, you recall, can be conditional or unconditional, highly specific or a more general pledge. Like scheduling time for God, setting the spiritual life down "in black and white" can be very helpful.

Undergirding this is the notion of spirituality as an attitude, as an outlook, according to Merton's brilliant concept. Making time for God is a part of our way of life, not a duty, an intrusion, or an unwanted interruption. We can make time for the many things we really want to do. Until we feel this way about vigils or prayer time, we must be patient with ourselves, and yet at the same time quietly firm. Without any solitude at all, Nouwen believes, the spiritual life cannot grow as it should.

However, most of us lead lives that do not reinforce the spiritual attitude—or the need for solitude in space and time. This means that our commitment to the spiritual life requires discipline on our part. Nouwen notes that we often meet such commitment with resistance. This was also a concern for Merton. Day-dreaming and drowsing are forms of resistance, Nouwen astutely adds. However, if we stay with the attitude and discipline, our resistance will diminish and we will come to treasure our times set aside for God.

How to Know You Are Never Alone

"We come to know not only with the mind but also with the heart, that we are really never alone." Gradually, Nouwen observes, we look forward to our quiet time with God. Even in depression, I believe we can maintain the spiritual outlook and discipline. "Appointments with God" help structure our day and "gradually, we begin to sense this hopeful presence of God in our lives" more consistently. In our vigils of depression, we can open our wounds to God's light, and eventually these very wounds may begin to look different. They may even become sources of healing.

"How can wounds become a source of healing?"

Henri Nouwen challenges us with this question in his classic book *The Wounded Healer*. This is an important question for us, as we deal with depression. Is this time of depression a total waste? Is there anything we can offer from it that we could not offer before? Is this a lost season, or is something learned, something gained?

Seeing Yourself as a Wounded Healer

Out of our own wounds, we can offer healing to others—this is one of Nouwen's hallmark beliefs. If we share our wounds, it is not as emotional or spiritual exhibitionism, but rather as an act of "hospitality" to another, in Nouwen's terms. By sharing our own wounds, we create a hospitable space for others to share theirs.

Depression is a wound to the spirit just as much as it is a medical illness; from our whole person, body, mind, and spirit, we can draw "hospitality" and support for others who suffer with any illness. "We grow strong in the broken places," wrote Ernest Hemingway. Perhaps this happens best when we share the broken places in the light of the cross.

The crucified God is the ultimate wounded healer. `By his wounds we are healed," Isaiah prophesies, and we look ahead to the risen Christ, radiant and yet still marked by his wounds. There is no incongruity here for most people who have endured serious depression, which always leaves internal marks. We feel well, we are well, but we remember. Our compassion has grown; our awareness of suffering links us to others in a new way. Life seems more precious to us .than ever. Perhaps this is so because of our scars, the remembrance of pain.

One day, you may be with another who is suffering through a depression. You may find the right time and place to share your own experience. Your attitude of "hospitality" may help the sufferer to share his wounds and open them to the light. Your presence may help her or him to feel less like a leper—less alone. A friend of mine was this presence for me; presence that I will never forget. Quiet support and "hospitality" are far more powerful than I imagined.

When you see yourself not only as the "walking wounded" but as an apprentice wounded healer, the axis of your whole world shifts. Your depression is not quite as useless as it seemed. You are not as disconnected as you thought.

Take the suffering you feel today and see it in another way: as clay on a potter's wheel, reshaped into a vessel to hold someone else's pain one day. Write it, reflect on it, ready it even as you live it out. God will draw some good from this wounded time, Nouwen believed, from a wealth of experience. This poem-prayer will echo for you when it comes your turn to be the wounded healer.

YOU ARE CHRIST'S HANDS
Christ has no body now on earth but yours
no hands but yours
no feet but yours.
Yours are the eyes through which is to look out
Christ's compassion to the world;
Yours are the feet with which he is to go about
doing good;
Yours are the hands with which he is to bless men
now
—Teresa of Avila

Harvesting Hope:
Julian of Norwich and
Therese of Lisieux

JULIAN OF NORWICH: FEELING LOVED JUST AS YOU ARE

Somewhat afraid, you come to her window.

They say she has powers, unusual gifts. Some say her name in hushed tones, and many say she draws her wisdom from her visions, so you come to her and tell her your need. When you finish there is a brief silence. Then it begins.

First, she places a tiny object in your palm.

Then, three sets of words she speaks, and one question.

Suddenly, you weep; the pain is gone.

Julian of Norwich was a holy woman; some called her a saint. You could turn to her with your secrets and troubles; she kept them safe, and if you told her about your depression, she would not condemn you or say your trouble was the devil's work, nor would she catechize you as the clergy would.

Instead, she would listen to you and then she would speak to you of God's love as you never heard before, not the God of wrath you have heard lately preached in the church. More wondrous, she would speak of God's love for you, even you—yes, you.

So you tell her the rest: This secret gnawing at you, keeping you from comfort and prayer. This is the shame of your heart: You have always felt too small, too lowly, too unimportant for God's concern, and so for years, you have been unable to pray. This must mean you are bad, maybe evil, and you could be burnt as a witch if you are found out; this could happen; the neighbors and clergy keep a close watch on personal piety. Still you can't help it, you feel so small. . . .

Regaining Your Personal Sense of Worth

Dame Julian listens calmly. She has seen the smoke rise from the marketplace when witches are burned. She sees many kinds of suffering from her window and hears of more, but she does not speak of them to you. Instead, she tells you about a tiny thing she saw in one of her visions. She saw a tiny thing, no bigger than a hazelnut. "I was amazed that it could last, for I thought that because of its littleness, it would suddenly have fallen to nothing. And I was answered in my understanding: it lasts and always will because. . ." (she puts the hazelnut into your hand). "God made it ... God loves it ... God preserves it."

You look at the tiny round shape on your palm.

"How, then," she asks, "how can *you* be too little for God?" That is when you weep; the pain is gone.

Gently, she continues: "God desires us to understand that along with great things, God is equally with small and simple things. We, too, should realize that the smallest thing will not be forgotten."

For anyone in depression, when we can feel so small and worthless, this is important to hear. If we have any thoughts of suicide or self-destructiveness, we can remember that we are unique, not expendable. We do not have to be great to matter to God, nor can we ever be too small.

Awakening the Wisdom of the Soul

Throughout the calamitous fourteenth century, people came to Dame Julian for wise spiritual counsel. One of the best known and best loved spiritual guides, her theology has had a strong revival in our own time. From this solitary English mystic, we hear a distinctive voice.

Julian, a Benedictine nun, became an anchoress, solemnly vowed to live until death in two rooms attached to her church, her life given over to prayer and spiritual counseling. One of her windows opened on the sanctuary, enabling her to participate at Mass. The other window opened on a busy street; here people came for counsel.

In 1373, during a severe illness and a "near-death" experience, Julian had twenty-four hours of mystical experiences, visions which she set down in her book *Revelations of Divine Love.* Her theology, based on these revelations, is hope-filled, unlike the prevailing view of a wrathful God, punishing wicked humanity with the Black Plague, the Hundred Years' War, and the Peasants' Revolt. Julian had been shown a different way.

Recovering Your Sense of Spiritual Joy

"You will yourself behold that all will be well and all manner of things will be well," Julian speaks the Lord's word to her. Today, this is one of Julian's most famous lines. In her age and ours, Julian's optimism is distinctive. Hers is a systematic theology of hope and joy—not facile joy, not "cheap grace," but the joy to which Jesus refers in his parables of wedding feasts.

Rejoice and be glad, Jesus tells us.

Rejoice in the Lord always, St. Paul exhorts us.

"Let us rejoice greatly that God dwells within us; and let us even more rejoice that we dwell in God," writes Julian.

Julian's holy joy was a light in an era of midnights. In depression it is always midnight as well. In historical and psychological midnights, Julian counters with a different attitude. Her optimism lifts the spirit without tricking the soul. Her optimism is realistic, tough enough to withstand the disasters and unrest around her.

For her, optimism and hope *do not* depend on our current surroundings. We can hope in God even in our present state of depression. Our current surroundings and present state, good or ill, are subject to change. Life itself is change—tilting toward hope.

Most important to her, however, is Jesus and his saving work of the cross. Jesus "suffered and died out of love.... And he *takes joy* in these deeds of his humanity" Here, joy and suffering are not mutually exclusive—once again, we see them intersect. In one image, Julian sees the crucifixion as an act of "Jesus as mother," whose agony on the cross was likened to birthing labor, in which he is *"bearing us for joy"* as into
new life.

Using the Power of Spiritual Presence

God's incomprehensible love is the ground of Julian's emphasis on joy and optimism. This love was revealed to her in her visions and she meditated on it for years. *"We are so preciously loved by God that we cannot even comprehend it,"* she wrote. "No created being can ever know how much and how sweetly and tenderly God loves them."

How are we to respond to this love?

With love, Julian would say. With joy. With prayer as a "loving gaze fixed on him," on Jesus. We do not always need words. The loving gaze comes from the heart. For us in depression, this is valuable "spiritual direction." Deep depression makes it hard to find and use words; if we cannot get out of bed, we are not likely to compose devotions. But no matter how we feel, we can offer prayer as a "gaze of love."

Julian therefore says:

Rejoice, You can never be too small for God.
Rejoice, God dwells in us and we dwell in God.
Rejoice, God clothes us with incomprehensible love.
This is how we give thanks to our Lord. It is easy to rejoice when times are easy; when times are hard, our joy is a sacrifice, an offering.

The wise woman of Norwich left us the gift of great optimism in a dark time. It seems right to honor Julian with a poem by thirteenth-century mystic Mechtild of Magdeburg (ca. 1259). Her visions took form as poetry, collected in *The Flowing Light of the Godhead.* For both holy women, "exuberance, too, was part of the mystic's path."

I CANNOT DANCE, 0 LORD, UNLESS
I cannot dance, 0 Lord,
Unless You lead me.
If you wish me to leap joyfully,
Let me see You dance and sing
Then I will leap into Love
And from Love into Knowledge,
And from Knowledge into the Harvest,
That sweetest Fruit beyond human sense.
There I will stay with You, whirling.

—Mechtild of Magdeburg

+++

ST. THERESE OF LISIEUX: LIVING LARGE, THE LITTLE WAY

"Be of good courage. Do not be afraid of your little failures. Our Lord does not look so much at the greatness of our actions . . . as at the love with which we do them. What then have we to fear?"

The voice of an ancient and wise holy soul, it seems. An abbess? A pope? This would make the speaker laugh, for she also had a sense of humor. St. Therese of Lisieux, often called the "Little Flower," never lived to be old or venerable, but she was wise. Her spiritual insight went far beyond her age; at only twenty-four, she died of tuberculosis. Although she never left the Carmelite convent she entered at fifteen, her autobiography, *The Story of a Soul,* has made her one of the greatest of Christian missionaries in history.

Therese's book has had tremendous effect on millions of readers and it still does. It reaches right into ordinary lives, offering lay people an accessible spiritual way—the "little way," as Therese herself called it. This way is available to everyone. It is simple, but not easy; for some it may be a great challenge.

The core of St. Therese's teaching is this: In the spiritual life, you must understand that you are like a small child in relation to God. This is the spiritual reality. God's love indwells "the simplest souls who welcome his grace as in those who are the most highly privileged," she writes. "He gives himself not just to the great, but to the little child...."

Here is an echo of Julian's teaching, which Therese did not know The two women, writing in different languages, centuries apart, have similar theology, dovetailing and complementing each other.

The Liberation of Leaning on God

"The Lord has created great saints who are the roses and the lilies of his kingdom, but he has also created lesser ones, simple daisies and violets growing at his feet." This might be a great blow to the ego, especially in an age that makes celebrities of its roses. This, of course, is no problem for us, the depressed. When this illness takes us over, there is no chance of feeling floral. We could not pretend to identify with anything sporting petals. No violets. No daisies. Moss—on our good days—that's close enough. Nonetheless, we are never too small, too worthless, too lowly for God. This is the wisdom of the "little way."

As Julian teaches with the image of a hazelnut, Therese uses the child-parent model. In this model, we are the child. These two great mystics squarely confront the issue of our creaturehood in relation to our Creator. They take on one of the most troublesome issues for humanity, a problem since the Garden *of* Eden: accepting that we *are not God*.

We are not the author of this play, says C. S. Lewis. We are the created and not the creator. God is the potter, and we are the clay, Jeremiah reminds us. For thousands of years, we have struggled with our creaturely status. Therese, however, in her lively, sympathetic voice, has presented it in a way that has been extraordinarily acceptable, yet not quick or easy or cheap. Using the image of a staircase, which we cannot climb all by ourselves, Therese insists that we take the first step. We are children, but we cannot be passive. "If you do not take that first step," she warns, "your stay on the ground will be a long one."

Therese teaches that it is our love for God that matters, not worldly success. Our society teaches us just the opposite. Ironically, the experience of depression helps us understand the Little Flower's teachings. When we are in depression, we know what it is to need God, to reach for that Power greater than ourselves—and greater than our depression.

Losing Your Dread of the Dark

"Do not be afraid of the dark," Therese would tell us if we consulted her about our depression and our sense of God's absence. "Do not complain that you cannot see him who carries you in his arms. Trust . . . the dark will lose its terrors." Depression reveals our relation to God, she might add. We understand that dependence on God is not weakness; in fact it requires perseverance and strength.

Therese never lost her sense of God's great love for us, nor did she fear death. Her love for God seemed to grow even stronger as her illness and suffering increased. She did not need a vision or sense of heaven to know it is there. Jesus may seem hidden, she says, but he will help us "without seeming to do so." As she weakened, her faith stayed strong. "Have no fear. He is at our side," she says. "We know he is there."

I NEVER saw a moor,
I never saw the sea;
Yet know I how the heather looks,
And what a wave must be.

I never spoke with God,
Nor visited in heaven;
Yet certain am I of the spot
As if the chart were given.

—Emily Dickinson

Standing Strong in Spirit: St. John of the Cross and St. Ignatius of Loyola

ST. JOHN OF THE CROSS: How You CAN LEARN TO SEE IN THE DARK

"Our spiritual ascent is a journey by night," the new guide briefs us. We will travel in darkness, climb at midnight, bring along almost nothing. There is no moon, there are no stars—just the blackness, the climb, and the guide; he alone knows the way. We were not encouraged to bring our own maps.

All this sounded exciting when we signed on, but now we nervously finger our checklist. This whole idea seems intimidating. Why didn't we look into it more carefully? This is not just an exercise for depression; this is also a stiff climb for the soul—a kind of Outward Bound venture on the spiritual landscape's steepest of slopes. The guide is renowned, but seems stern, severe. Again, he says: "Our spiritual ascent is a journey by night. Faith is our only light in the hours after midnight.... We move toward God not by understanding ... not by what we can feel or imagine, but by belief ... by faith."

St. John of the Cross is indeed a rigorous guide, one of the West's greatest spiritual masters and author of *The Dark Night of the Soul*, which sees God's work in us through darkness, not light. He is, in a way, like a great coach who urges us on to stretch the limits, to push ourselves a bit and refuse to give up—and all the way, he encourages us. All the way, as he leads us, his love for God outweighs all else.

Discovering New Freedom in the Darkness

At a certain point in the spiritual journey, John teaches, God will draw a person into a deeper faith. In this stage, we are called to a new level of spiritual experience: "darkness" in prayer, a dearth of images or sensations or an awareness of God's presence. If we persevere in this way, we are actually liberated from any dependence on anything other than faith in God who is with us in the darkness, whether we feel this or not. Often, in the spiritual life, we expect "big moments," images, revelations, out-of-body experiences, and other sensations. We invite disappointment if we don't get what we want.

If we do not feel God's presence, we may assume that God is distant, cold, no longer caring about us—"Deus *absconditus,"* the hidden God. At this point, many prayers and seekers turn away with a sense of rejection and failure. It is at this point, however, when we can reach a deeper level of prayer or meditation. If you have a meditation time with no "big moments," that is not failure. If you endure, it is faith.

One of the "dark night's" great values is freedom. We realize that God's presence with us is not measured by our sense of it. This liberates us from feeling rejected or distanced from God. Instead, we can know God's ongoing presence, as two spouses know they love each other while they are apart. In relation to God, John would urge us to depend on nothing else but faith and hope and, above all, love. He writes of God's love as a "divine fire" which purifies the soul so that God may be united with the soul by God's "sweet, peaceful and glorious love. . . ."

A mystic, reformer, a great poet, John was above all a man of faith, even when he ran afoul of his superiors and did much of his work in prison. He also sustained a long warm friendship with St. Teresa of Avila and wrote impassioned poetry to God. Along with his great faith, he prized hope. "The more we come to rely on hope, and the deeper our hope, the stronger our union with God will be," he writes. "We ascend to God through hope."

Courage to Carry You Through Darkness

Depression challenges our capacity for faith and hope. Relief and restoration take time, as noted. Nothing legitimate works in one session or one day. Like me, you may have to try different approaches before you find the right one. During my last depression, I read the work of people who overcame depression after long searches. Their companionable words bolstered my shaky faith in getting well.

I read these books several times. Their authors recovered, but I began to doubt that their stories could apply to me. My depression was resistant, "refractory" in clinical terms. So far, certain medications had helped me but for a short time, then lost their effect. This was a challenge to my doctors, but they reassured me. At that point I had to muster my faith in them. I could do that. It was not hard to have faith in others. Having faith in myself— that was something else. This time, I felt, I had used up all my resilience.

What sustained me was a small stubborn faith that God would not leave me. This string of faith had surprising strength. I could give up on myself—but something in me could not give up on God. Something within me hoped in God, no matter what.

Defying logic, emotion, intuition, my spirit kept right on clinging to God. On my part, there was no conscious exercise of will, virtue, or courage; I take no credit. That string of faith refused to break. In my mind, it looked like ordinary white string, sturdy and serviceable, and that was all. No shining imagery, no angels. String. It unreeled, straight, and strong, from some height or depth beyond my sight. I did not dare to analyze it. There are times, St. John says, when you do nothing except receive what God gives, and stay out of God's way. There is more than darkness: there is the purifying fire of God's love working in your soul, warming, wooing, winning you forever.

> DARK NIGHT [excerpt]
> O night, my guide!
> O night more friendly than the dawn!
> O tender night that tied
> lover and the loved one,
> loved one and the lover fused.

—St. John of the Cross

+++

ST. IGNATIUS OF LOYOLA: SUMMONING YOUR SPIRITUAL STRENGTH TO KNOW YOUR ENEMY

Know his ways and how he wounds you.

The enemy infiltrates your front lines, attacking by stealth, stirring within you, "darkness of the soul, turmoil of the mind, disturbances and temptations which lead to loss of faith, loss of hope, loss of love. The soul finds itself completely apathetic, tepid, sad, and separated as it were, from its Creator and Lord."

This is the voice of a soldier turned saint: Ignatius of Loyola, in his *Spiritual Exercises,* "one of the most important documents in the history of Christian spirituality . . . a book of discipline which teaches the life of the Spirit . . ." (quoted in Foster, *Devotional Classsics,* p. 225).

Another great Spanish mystic and spiritual genius, in 1540 Ignatius was the founder of the historic and elite order of the Society of Jesus, known more frequently as Jesuits. A keen observer of human emotions, Ignatius offers spiritual wisdom that transfers remarkably well to depression. If the enemy is considered depression, Ignatius is the spiritual warrior at our side, winning the battle.

"The enemy will lose courage and take flight as soon as a person .. . stands courageously . . . and does exactly the opposite of what the enemy expects," says this self-declared "soldier for Christ." The enemy, he continues, is like a military leader who attacks at your weakest point. If you lose courage in the midst of the battle and take flight, "the enemy will pursue ferociously."

Taking Control When You Feel Tepid

Whether you think of the enemy as Satan or depression, the analogy works. St. Ignatius uses many vivid analogies and visualizations in his *Exercises* and retreats. He wants us to feel the immediacy of Christ's life and death in the present, not only the past. As we listen for the voice of Jesus in our lives, the Ignatian way helps us to hear it, now, today. Ignatius accomplishes this with insightful imagery, and, in his treatment of desolation, his counsel continues to be strangely pertinent to depression.

"Darkness of soul, turmoil, loss of hope, a soul apathetic, sad, tepid. . . ." This may be intended for desolation, but it also sounds like notes on depression on any chart. Ignatius' voice is brisk and bracing. He makes it seem possible to stand strong and resolute against depression (in *conjunction with treatment),* but what about this state called "tepid," also on Thomas Merton's list of warning signs?

From a spiritual perspective, tepid or half-hearted prayer can lead to apathy and other problems. From an emotional perspective, however, that lukewarm feeling means something quite specific to me. It means I am slipping. Almost imperceptibly, I am sliding away from health toward depression. Tepid can feel like resignation, loss of motivation, a sense of aloneness, and a vague dread that life may be pointless. If this outlook lasts and grows more oppressive, the dread "darkness of soul" could be next. This "tepid" sign is so sneaky, you may ignore it—a big mistake. The Greek Furies are coming in for a landing.

St. Ignatius gives us a sense of strength that we can summon when warning signals come. Perhaps, at times, we can avert or diminish a full-blown episode with medical input, or whatever works for you: cognitive behavior therapy exercises, physical exercise, protein, vitamins, or we can try out a sassy in-your-face attitude toward depression. This stance would be compatible with cognitive behavior therapy, noted in the appendix, which works with thought patterns and helps depressed people try to function.

Views differ about attitude and depression. In acute or major depression attitude is not enough, but we should not give up on it altogether. Some experts would argue for it, some against. Whatever your view on attitude, it can *banish the fear of depression.* Attitude can dispel the dread of a new depressive episode, speeding toward us like an oncoming car in our lane at night. This anti-dread stance is a good thing to master. *Depression with attitude;* it's worth a try.

Whatever happens, whether depression comes on or not, we turn to our spiritual resources. St. Ignatius calls us stand in God's strength, not our own. The center of the spiritual life, for Ignatius, is the union of our will with God's will. Toward the end of his celebrated *Exercises* there is a beautiful example of the Ignatian view, presented as a prayer:

> *Take, 0 Lord, and receive all my liberty, my memory, my understanding and my entire will, all that I have and possess. Thou hast given all these things to me; to Thee, 0 Lord, I restore them: all are Thine, dispose of them according to Thy will. Give me Thy love and Thy grace, for this is enough for me.*

This prayer is so powerful, you might consider memorizing it, particularly the last line. When St. Ignatius says that we stand in God's strength, he means giving all that we are into God's keeping. This is not loss of self, as some fear, but union with our source. Thus, there we stand, awed by the great man's great faith. We stand clutching our little faith like a coin-purse and wonder if this is really enough.

St. Ignatius of Loyola does not measure our faith or demand that we do so. His *Exercises* are for Christians whose faith needs to grow Faith is always a good offering—and who can truly measure it but the One who loves us the most and stands with us in our need?

In vigil, in depression, in desolation, St. Ignatius gives us a ringing reminder of the presence and power of God all around us. We don't have to face "the enemy" unarmed and alone; instead, we call on God's strength—and in that strength, have faith, even if our faith seems puny, paltry, like my image of common white string.

Ignatius, in his books and his *Exercises,* is very clear that Jesus Christ is to be known now, not as a figure off in the past. The saving action of Jesus is not restricted by space or time or our strength. If we can hold on to him in faith, no matter how small, no matter what happens, we have the greatest of victories.

SMALL WIRE
My faith
is a great weight
hung on a small wire....
God does not need
too much wire to keep Him there,
just a thin vein,
with blood pushing back and forth in it,
and some love.
As it has been said:
Love and a cough
cannot be concealed.
Even a small cough.
Even a small love.
So if you have only a thin wire,
God does not mind. . . .

—Anne Sexton

Love as Language:
St. Catherine of Siena and
Mother Teresa of Calcutta

ST. CATHERINE OF SIENA: SINGING LESSONS
FOR SILENT VOICES

Beyond the high wall, a voice is singing—spilling prayers on the air, scattering them like handfuls of silver. Then the stern convent bells take command. The garden falls silent. Until tomorrow, the singer is gone.

The voice belonged to St. Catherine of Siena, a Dominican tertiary at eighteen whose sung devotions were overheard as she walked alone in the convent garden. Otherwise, she was deeply contemplative, a mystic and visionary since girlhood. In 1366, when she was nearly twenty, she had a life-changing mystical experience, leading her into service out in the world.

"Our Holy Mother," they called her, the poor and the sick, the most unwanted, the worst cases: plague, leprosy, and cancer. All her life, however, she remained a mystic and visionary, describing her revelations as she dictated the story of her life with God, *Dialogo*.

Finding the Inner Cell of the Soul

She speaks of "the inner cell," where she encounters God in the deep silence of her soul. "The more I enter, the more I find, and the more I find, the more I see of Thee," she wrote to her Lord, but being spiritually wise and generous, she knew her gifts were for others.

"Loving me and loving your neighbor are inseparable," God's word came to her. For her, at times, this took the form of political action. Her insights were so valued, she settled city conflicts and counseled popes, still maintain-

219

ing her life of prayer. One of the few women doctors of the church, she is also the patron saint of Italy.

St. Catherine's way was firmly based on a theology of love. "Nails would not have held the God-man fast to the cross, had not love held him there," she said in her *Dialogo*. Her life was an extraordinary weave of intense mysticism and demanding service, despite her own frequent bouts with illness. All she did rose from her passionate sense of God's love for all of humanity.

Learning to Speak God's Language

For St. Catherine, love is the language God speaks to us. It is a language we need to hear in depression, sometimes desperately, when depression makes us feel unlovable. As we seem to fall into inner darkness, she says, God reaches for us. "Nor will you ever fall into darkness," she tells us. Look into God's heart and see the unspeakable love for you there. "Then the soul, seeing how much she is loved, is herself filled to overflowing."

If you came to St. Catherine for aid with depression, she would speak of God's love for you, as a word of the Lord: "Turn where you will; you will find nothing but my mercy. I reach out to my creatures, to sinner and saint alike. My mercy overcomes sin and death. . . . On earth it is the language with which I speak to you."

Then she would challenge you with a question: Why are you trying to walk through the water?

The central image for Catherine is a "tempestuous river," spanned by a bridge. We must make a crossing, but we have a choice: take the bridge or go through the river. She well understands the presence and power of the river, a barrier that stalls or stops us on our way.

Depression can be like a river, sweeping us into swift, deepening waters. We get so caught up in it, we can do nothing but struggle. Like a river's strong, treacherous currents, our feelings can overwhelm us: fear, self-hatred, and aloneness. "You are not alone," Catherine wants us to know, through God's word: "I loved you before you existed, and knowing this you can place your trust in my love and set aside every fear."

Set aside every fear. Trust my love.

Such love is powerful. It makes a way where there is none. It transforms; it frees. It is God's love that built the bridge for us over the river. Catherine, presenting the *bridge as Christ* himself, conveys to us a powerful spiritual message.

Christ laid down his life for us on the cross: "No one has greater love than this, to lay down one's life for one's friends" (John 15:13). But Catherine teaches that *Christ continually lays down his life for us,* just as a bridge and road are continually laying themselves out before us, always there, always waiting. In Catherine's vision, a spiritual bridge is built to repair the connection, broken by sin, between God and humankind. It is pure gift. "Never forget that I give you everything out of my love for you."

Dare to Take the Bridge

In light of this love, we might rethink the river. If we have resisted God, perhaps we relent. If we resist our depression, perhaps we seek treatment. Perhaps our attitude changes and we decide to live through or with or in spite of depression. We might stop struggling in the water and finally come up for air.

We just might dare to take the bridge. St. Catherine is eager for us to do so because she knows the way is good. However, taking that first step is up to us, as it was in the spirituality of St. Therese. Such a step is the classic leap of faith. In St. Catherine's thought, it is a leap of connection.

Connection: this is what Catherine's way is about. In her own life she fuses the lives of the spirit and service. She creates bridges between feuding cities and citizens; she moves between powerful popes and the poorest of the poor. Above all, she calls us back to connection with God—God, the destination; God, the bridge. But how do we do this? How can we make this connection?

Choose it, St. Catherine would say. Pray it, live it.

"If you choose me as your companion," God's word comes, "you will not be alone; my love will always be with you.... Your soul unites itself with me by acts of love ... nurtured in prayer." What delight awaits you; no words can express it, says St. Catherine, whose voice once rose from a hidden garden, a voice singing prayers in the language of love.

PRAYER 20 [excerpt]
We were enclosed,
O eternal Father,
Within the garden of your breast.
You drew us out of your holy mind
Like a flower. . . .
I have nothing to give but what you have given me.

—St. Catherine of Siena

+++

MOTHER TERESA OF CALCUTTA: SOMETHING BEAUTIFUL FOR GOD

"You can do what I can't do. I can do what you can't do. Together we can do something beautiful for God." She invites us into partnership, this saint for our times, Mother Teresa of Calcutta.

Founder of the Missionaries of Charity and Nobel Laureate, her life has certain parallels with that of St. Catherine of Siena. Like Catherine, Teresa felt moved to leave her convent to work on the streets with the poor. In 1948, she began her ministry in India, caring for the sick and "the poorest of the poor." As her ministry spread to five continents and her new order grew to four thousand, she continued to ground all her actions in prayer. "Prayer feeds the soul as blood feeds the body," she writes.

Seeing the Face of Jesus in Others

Mother Teresa saw the poor as the embodiment of Christ in our world, and in each dying person she plucked from the street, she saw his face. If we feel disconnected from the biblical Jesus, if his life seems too long ago, too far away, perhaps we are not looking for him, very often, in others.

In all suffering people, Mother Teresa always saw Jesus "in their distress and disguise." She wanted to help the suffering feel God's love. When we are in depression, we are the suffering. In us, Mother Teresa would see Christ and she would see our lives as precious. She would want to help us feel God's love. Somewhere, in each of us, God is at work and we must let that work continue.

If Mother Teresa would see value in us, perhaps we can try to discern it in ourselves, but can we really be expected to see with Teresa's eyes? We are not saints. We are not holy. Isn't it absurd to think so? No! Teresa would answer with spirit. A young man once came up to her in an airport. "Are you a saint?" he asked. "Yes," she said, jabbing his chest with her finger, "and so are you!"

We do not think of ourselves that way, though the term was used for the faithful in the early church. "Holiness is not a luxury for the few; it is not just for some people. It is meant for you and for me, for all of us...."

Mother Teresa was emphatic. "To be holy does not mean to do extraordinary things.... Holiness is simply belonging to God."

The Current and the Wire

Mother Teresa's imagery is like a modern version of St. Catherine's bridge. Now the bridge is electronic. "Often you see electric wires .. electric cables, useless until the current passes through them.... The wire is you and me." Mother Teresa again draws us into a partnership. "The current is God. We have the power to let the current pass through us, to produce the light of the world, or we can refuse, and allow the darkness to spread."

We have this power, even in depression. We can work with small images, in small stages, one at a time. We can picture light from a lamp, or a light in a window of our own house, and we can still picture the vigil candles in a church or cathedral. God sends his current through us, even us.

This imagery can help us with a depression-related "disease." We may suffer from it as an offshoot of depressive illness. Mother Teresa often said that we now have medicine for leprosy and tuberculosis and many other ills. The neglected disease is epidemic, and its treatment varies. It is what Mother Teresa calls the disease of "unwantedness."

Winning Out Over "Unwantedness"

When we are depressed, we are susceptible to this feeling. We may think of ourselves as useless, unacceptable—no one would want us when we are depressed. We may even reject ourselves. As long as we do, we cannot be of much use to others.

At those times, we might remember that Mother Teresa urged us to "make the unwanted know they are loved—and they are wanted. God is within them." Can we apply this idea to ourselves when depression confronts us? If so, we begin to reconnect with "the power house" of God.

Depression, for us, often leads to a great sense of disconnection. Withdrawal is a classic symptom of depression—we retreat from others, activities, life itself. We also may feel disconnected from God, who must be disappointed in us. The assumption may be that God breaks the connection, but this is something we do ourselves. Teresa calls us to reconnect.

Connection for Catherine appears as a bridge; connection for Teresa is electricity. In Italy and India, six hundred years apart, these two women inspire us to seek reconnection—with God, with neighbor, with those we love. How? Prayer is a universal connection with God. It appears in each window of this chapel, even in lives so active as St. Catherine's and Mother Teresa's. "Everything starts with prayer," said Teresa. "If we pray, we will be able to love, and if we love, we will be able to serve."

To serve, we do not have to go very far. Mother Teresa suggests that we ask ourselves if we know the poor. In our own families, among our friends, are there people who are poor *not* because they lack food? "You will find Calcutta all over the world if you have eyes to see," Mother Teresa reminds us. *If we have eyes to see.* In depression, we may see ourselves among the poor.

If we, as the poor, the sick, came to Mother Teresa, she would remind us, however unwanted, however poor, however depressed we feel, that we are always wanted by God. God's spirit flows and God has a purpose for each one of us. Mother Teresa would say this: If God can love throwaways on the streets of Calcutta, how could God reject you?

She might remind you about electricity. Are we connected to the "powerhouse," as she says when she uses this image for God. No? You can reconnect. The current can hum through the wires again. In any form of depression, even severe ones, we can slowly begin to picture the wires, the light coming on. A small image. A start. We can picture the light coming on in our room, in our eyes. More small images of a great hope. To these small images, we can hold fast.

"We can only do small things with great love," said Mother Teresa. We can do small things in depression. We can love; we can form new attitudes and new images.

"You can do what I can't do. I can do what you can't do," Mother Teresa invites us again. "Together we can do something beautiful for God."

CHRISTMAS POOR
You are the caller.
You are the poor.
You are the stranger at my door.
You are the wanderer,
the unfed.
You are the homeless
with no bed.

You are the man
driven insane.
You are the child
crying in pain.

You are the other who comes to me;
if I open to another you're born in me.

—Anonymous Celtic Prayer

Why Not Now?:
St. Augustine of Hippo
and Rick Moody

ST. AUGUSTINE OF HIPPO: LET IT BE NOW, LET IT BE NOW

"Too late have I loved you, 0 beauty of ancient days, yet ever new! Too late have I loved you! And behold, you were within, and I abroad, and there I searched for you. . . . You were with me but I was not with you. . . ."

This has the sound of a passionate love letter—and that is exactly what it is. St. Augustine, a passionate soul, wrote this letter to God, who turned out to be the great love of his life, though he had loved before. Augustine, one of Christianity's greatest figures, shaping our faith as theologian, author, bishop, doctor of the church, was once a worldly man, and then an anguished man whose fourth-century struggle sounds curiously modern.

His famous *Confessions,* the first spiritual autobiography, traces his progress from sinner to saint. As an adult he followed his father's non-Christian perspective, studied the philosophers, dined well, kept mistresses, and lived unmarried with a woman who bore him a son, and yet, none of this was enough for him. Passionately drawn to a dedicated celibate Christian life, he struggled to make this change, and yet he could not do it.

Moving Out of a House Divided

"I was a house divided against itself," he said of himself. Again and again, he moved toward a new life, then pulled back. Deeply ashamed of his sins and his past, striving to let go of his current attachments, he was

227

in torment: "In my heart I kept saying, 'Let it be now, let it be now!'"

Finally, he wept. "I kept crying, `How long shall I go on saying, "Tomorrow, tomorrow?" Why not now?"

Augustine heard children nearby, calling to each other: "Take it and read, take it and read!" He opened the Bible and saw the passage that decided him: "Put on the Lord Jesus Christ and make no more provisions for the flesh ..." (Romans 13:13). His inner darkness left him; he felt light and peace.

These spiritual turning points appear in many of the "windows" in this metaphorical chapel. St. Catherine and Mother Teresa were called out into active service, while Julian was called in as an anchoress. Ignatius and Merton made dramatic departures from their old lives, one military, one hedonistic. Our life-changes may not be so dramatic or clear, but we too pass through seasons. Illness is a season unto itself, a season of mist and wind, drawing on faith and on our capacity for transformation.

Tracking the Spirit's Transformations

If depression's season runs long, we may become weary of walking against the wind. It's too much, too long, too hard; we're done. If we have gone through several medication trials, we may want to give up. If we remain in therapy but see no progress, we may want to quit. In treatment or not, we might feel exhausted from the everyday struggle.

Sometimes, we struggle with God, angry that healing seems withheld. With St. Augustine, we cry out, "Let it be now, let it be now." It is vitally important for us to make the choice to be well, to hang on, to stay with treatment or find another that makes a better fit. Like St. Augustine, we must keep trying. Resist the temptation to think, "No one can help me, nothing can help me, this is my lot."

In some ways, it is easier to give in to such thinking. The courage and will to keep struggling can be agonizingly hard; St. Augustine's persistent struggle can encourage us, especially when results are slow.

When Augustine came to the height of his torment, he imagined a figure who beckoned to him and led him across the barrier, pointing out to him others who had done the same. "Can you not do what these men and women do?" he was asked. "Do you think they find the strength in themselves and not in the Lord their God? Why do you try to stand in your own strength and fail? Cast yourself upon him without fear, for he will welcome you and cure you of your ills." Soon after this, he took up the Bible and found his freedom.

A Woman Called Moses

Augustine's visualization encapsulates the transitions that come with the spiritual life. The first barrier is crossed when we begin—here, where we are, considering a new spiritual direction. The crossing of barriers is a strong motif in the Bible and in the spiritual life. We may delay, but the barrier waits.

There is an almost uncanny similarity between Augustine's visualization and the vision of a very different mystic: Harriet Tubman, an African-American slave in antebellum Maryland. Since childhood, she wanted freedom, but she was thirty when she ran away. Once free, she sensed God calling her to rescue other slaves. In the 1850s, she led three hundred slaves north, earning her the code-name "Moses."

Tubman was a devout Christian, visionary, and mystic. She talked with God every day "as with a friend," and God called her to freedom through a vision: "I'd be flying over cotton fields and cornfields and the corn was ripe. . . . I'd come to a river and fly over that. I'd come to a hill and fly over that. But I'd always get to a barrier and I couldn't fly across it. It would appear like I didn't have the strength, but just as I was sinking down, there'd be ladies in white over there, and they'd put out their hands and pull me across."

Crossing Your Barriers

Depression is a barrier to cross, like St. Catherine's river. We cross it in so many different ways—by seeking treatment, staying with treatment, working with depression, in vigil and prayer. After depression, the act of starting life again is also an act of crossing-over, because you are not quite the same; life itself is not quite the same.

With Augustine, we stand "trembling at the barrier," as he said, as we consider the vigil tradition and, in a larger sense, we consider commitment to a more spiritual outlook on our lives. St. Augustine speaks for us as he cries out:

"How long shall I go on saying, 'Tomorrow, tomorrow?'"

For love, he asked and answered, *Why not now?*

GOD SPEAKS TO THE SOUL
And God said to the soul:
I desired you before the world began,
I desire you now and you desire me.
And where the desires of two come together,
There love is perfected.
—Mechtild of Magdeburg

HOW THE SOUL SPEAKS TO GOD
Lord, you are my lover; My longing,
My flowing stream,
My sun,
And I am your reflection.
—Mechtild of Magdeburg

+++

RICK MOODY: THE PRAYER OF DESPERATION

On the adult floor of the psychiatric hospital, a youngish man played checkers and discovered prayer. A companion mentioned an aversion to kneeling, and to pray, Rick Moody soon realized, in a spiritual sense, you had to get down on your knees. "The prayer that comes first to all who learn to pray in earnest is the *prayer of desperation,*" he wrote, and by that time, desperation was his state.

After ten years of drifting and drugs, Moody was in treatment for depression in this hospital in Queens, and on the Fourth of July, sat with two nurses, a scarred, self-mutilated patient, and a radio. A song from Moody's childhood came on: "Candle in the Wind." The song was evocative. "I thought back on how far I had fallen since I was a kid...I was full of promise." Now he was here, wrecked, depressed, surrounded with half-ruined lives. Suddenly, as he thought back, a rare thing happened to him:

"I wept. In front of the others. I wept."

Hitting Bottom

"And then I prayed. I prayed solitarily, and later in the room I shared. . . . I prayed over meals, whenever there was a spare second. . . . I prayed the prayer of desperation. *God,* I prayed, *whoever you are, get me out of this. . . .*"

Rick Moody would be the first to say he is not a saint or mystic, but he belongs here because, as it happens, Rick Moody is a special spiritual guide. Like Merton, he is unflinchingly honest about his earlier life and genuine in his approach to spirituality. His is a contemporary voice that speaks directly to us, and like Merton, he goes straight to the bone. Like many growing up in comfortable secularity in the sixties, seventies, and eighties, Moody learned to pray before he believed.

"Belief wasn't something I or my peers believed in," he writes. "What was a spiritual need and how does prayer gratify or articulate it? It took me a long time to formulate compelling answers to these questions." But the spiritual need is compelling, universal, and demands its answers.

Since the sixties, it has been easier to meet that need with "recreational drugs." *(Not* antidepressants, which are completely different.) Moody and others his age found deceptive "answers" by getting high. At the end of a ten-year "spree of primitive liberty," he found himself in depression and in the hospital, although "doing drugs" and depression are not linked.

Tell Me You Are There

As he went on in prayer, he began discussing it with friends. It turned out that they were praying, too, and it was helpful. He talked with a producer in southern California who prayed throughout the devastating Oakland fires. Another friend confided that she would wake and simply murmur to God, "Help me." Another, a prominent magazine editor, adapted St. Augustine's prayer, "Whisper in my heart, tell me you are there."

Tell me you are there.

The question of "you" was not a problem.

Moody prayed without a clear concept of God; in some ways, by coincidence, his spirituality at that time bordered on the "Dark Night" of John of the Cross. Moody prayed without a sense of God's presence; with a sense of God's silence. At first, that's how it was: silence met with silence. Gradually, however, he found a new perspective: "Silence, it turns out, is redemptive, is generous." He also discovered silence itself as a form of relationship with God. Moody persisted in this silence and prayer.

Prayer Works

"When I got out of the hospital, when I was living alone in a converted filling station in Hoboken, New Jersey, when I was showing up for work and little else, when I was still suffering, in spite of medication ... then, though I had never gotten down on my knees. . . for anyone or anything, although I had never admitted the possibility that I could not solve my problems myself ... then I began to pray. Regularly." His prayers were simple and honest, no frills or complex forms about them. In fact, he prayed as Mother Teresa suggested: "Talk to God." Moody talked: *Give me a chance, please.*

The former psychiatric patient and "substance abuser" does not see prayer as "cheap grace" or some new kind of trip. Far from it. He agrees with William James, in *The Varieties of Religious Experience,* that prayer is an actual process which generates energy, where real work is actually being done that produces effects.

Start Where You Are, As You Are

Moody did not wait until he had some kind of theology figured out. He prayed as he was, where he was, and gradually he began to notice that he was feeling better. He even "passed some days without hopelessness." Anyone who has battled depression understands how stupendous such days can seem. To have one day, just one, without pain or hopelessness becomes a gift.

Moody's approach is one we might consider as we keep vigil. To have a spiritual life, he did not wait to find answers to all his spiritual questions. Instead of waiting or devising intellectual constructs, Moody prayed. Like Merton, prayer for him is an attitude and not a method.

Part of this attitude about the Divine is this: "You'll know it when you see it." It's like falling in love. You know it when it happens. And, Moody adds, "if it ain't broke, don't fix it." His prayer life did not break down; it grew stronger. Most mornings, sometimes on the subway or on planes or "in the silence before a movie starts," he engages in the dialogue of prayer and the practice of "listening" in meditation.

These days, he is well-read in the field of spirituality, a field in which he has become unpretentiously fluent. He is also the co-editor of *Joyful Noise: The New Testament Revisited,* and the author of three books, one of which, *The Ice Storm,* became a movie. Also, these days he prays for others; he prays for prayer. He prays that "the expressions of humility and joy and acceptance that are at the heart of the language of prayer will again be valuable on a larger scale."

Prayer and Recovery From Depression

In Moody's case, it seems, prayer had a strong effect on his recovery from depression. "I pray, therefore, because prayer works," he says; however, though he began to pray out of sheer desperation, he continued long after his desperation faded. Prayer for him was not a stopgap or a form of "jailhouse religion"; it was part of his life. Although he continued to read widely on the subject, he never reduced it to an analytic study. Like his first prayers, his continuing prayers came from the heart, from that "need within us for humility and joy and acceptance," along with our need for the hope and peace that the world cannot give.

In our quick-fix age, certain states cannot be "accessed" from the web or the world. There is no "virtual peace of mind." Depression strips so much away from us, scrapes off so much of our paint; we note peace of mind, the genuine article, in a new way. This is, of course, the hard way to learn. I do not recommend it. It doesn't make us better people, but it changes many things. After a depression, we are keenly aware of what the world can and cannot give. It can bring success and pleasure, power and happiness. These are good, but they may not be enough. Only God can give vision and meaning, lasting joy and courage, and the peace that passes understanding, the peace of Christ. At a certain point, we may find ourselves praying first for God's presence, simply to be with God as God is with us. Or, as Moody does, you may pray on behalf of prayer itself.

"I pray sometimes," Rick Moody writes, "for a renaissance in this ancient discourse, because the mysteries engendered by prayer are inspiring to behold." Inspiration seems to be in short supply in the rush of life, unless we are the poets or the saints—or recovering from depression, when everything looks slightly different, striking, brighter, sharper, and more fragile than before.

God Turns Up Everywhere

This is how it happens: One day, we begin to feel a little better, maybe two and three days in a row. Even with inevitable off-days, we go on improving, slowly, gingerly. We remember how we felt the week or month before—now, by contrast, the world comes into focus with a piercing clarity.

God's presence seems to turn up everywhere, coming through small things we have never witnessed quite this way: the fearless leaps of bottle corks and cats and toasted bread. Pale onions piled like giant pearls at a market. The slender arms of newly planted trees, the antic laugh of an old friend, and the animated FedEx man who always says, "God bless you."

God's voice sings at every window.

As the man wrote: "It's all around us."

GOD'S GRANDEUR

The earth is charged with the glory of God!
It will flame out like shining from shook foil;
It gathers to a greatness, like the ooze of oil...
And for all this, nature is never spent;
There lives the dearest freshness deep down things;
And though the last lights of the black West went
Oh, morning, at the brown brink eastward springs—
Because the Holy Ghost over the bent
World broods with warm breast and with ah! Bright
    wings.
    —Gerard Manley Hopkins

Yesterday is gone.
Tomorrow has not yet come.
We have only today.
Let us begin.
    —Mother Teresa of Calcutta

Appendix: Approaches to the Treatment of Depression

The "first-line treatment for most people with depression today consists of . . . medication, psychotherapy, or the combination" (Potter, et al., Depression Guideline Panel, 1993). My personal experience reflects this finding, with strong emphasis on medication. What is right for me, however, may not be right for you. Treatments vary with each individual. Here, in brief, are some of your options. I made short comments where I had something to add.

THE HOLISTIC APPROACH

This appeals to people who prefer to manage depression on their own. Strategies may include herbs (such as St. John's Wort), high doses of B vitamins, fish oil, and certain amino acids; acupuncture, reflexology, and massage; light boxes for seasonal depression; yoga or Tai Chi; meditation and creative visualization.

Comment: This approach did not work for me. My depression is too severe and resistant for this strategy, but it might be helpful for people with mild depressions. It is important to use herbs with care.

PSYCHO-PHARMACOLOGY

It is tremendously important to *find a psychiatrist experienced with psycho-pharmacology.* It may take several drug try-outs to find what works best for you. Do *not give up.* This is crucial. I remember wanting to quit more than once. Stay with it. Most side effects are worth it. You may need a combination of medications. The right one can be life-changing.

Comment: This is my treatment of choice, my highest recommendation. However, a new study, appearing in the *New England Journal of Medicine,* shows that a combination of medication and psychotherapy is more effective than either one alone. It changed my life. If you hate medication you may resist; I hope you can try this approach anyway. Look for a seasoned psycho-pharmacologist through an institute like NIH (National Institute of Health), Johns Hopkins in Baltimore, or Massachusetts General in Boston.

Important note: Antidepressants *do not* make you high or euphoric, nor do they turn you into someone else. The medications simply restore you to normal brain chemistry and real life.

PSYCHOTHERAPEUTIC APPROACH

As noted above, the Surgeon General's 1999 report recommends this as a first-line treatment, alone or with medication, and as noted above, a new study, appearing in the *New England Journal of Medicine,* views the combination of both as the best approach. Therapy can help with unresolved issues and repressed emotions. A gifted therapist is worth the search, and the support of that relationship can be healing in itself. A therapist who works with medication is helpful.

Comment: I found traditional therapy somewhat helpful, integrated therapy more so. The effectiveness of this approach depends largely on the therapist. However, my bias is clear: medication is important. Many therapists do pharmacology as well, or work with psychiatrists who do.

ELECTROCONVULSIVE SHOCK THERAPY

This approach remains somewhat controversial. Because it works quickly, it is often used in acute suicidal depressions, or in very severe depressions that are unresponsive to any other treatment. ECT induces a controlled grand mal seizure, which seems to rebalance the brain's chemistry. Treatment usually is a course of six to ten sessions. It can be done on an outpatient basis in most cases. Almost always there is some short-term memory loss which eventually returns.

Comment: I have no personal experience with this form of therapy, but I have read books by two respected therapists who themselves were treated with ECT for depression. Their experiences were positive and encouraging, dispelling some myths.

COGNITIVE THERAPY

This approach focuses on thought process. Techniques are taught for replacing irrational thoughts with new realistic ones, and changing "negative self-talk." This theory asserts that thoughts can be reprogrammed; in turn, they change feelings and brain chemistry. Cognitive principles of habit-formation are applied. Several experts offer books to work with at home (see Reading and Reference List), or you might look for a cognitive therapist.

Comment: I have worked with cognitive therapy and found it minimally helpful. For me, psychotherapy was more helpful. For me and many others, when brain chemistry is imbalanced, it is almost impossible to think clearly or concentrate (classic symptoms, as noted), and cognitive therapy deals with thoughts. This option may be best for milder depressions. CT is frequently used as a treatment for phobias.

DEVELOPING NEW SOLUTIONS

As I write, clinical trials are being conducted for a device something like a pacemaker, inserted into the chest. This device works with the vagus nerve to counteract depression and, so far, results are cautiously positive.

Your choice of treatment is very personal and individual. Once you make a selection, give it a good try to see if it feels right for you. If so, you will need to give it some time to begin to take effect. In any of these areas, most of the time, relief rarely comes quickly, but relief does come. I went through several medication trials, and there was a time when I thought I would never feel well again.

I stopped praying for healing, and prayed instead for strength to live with depression: a good prayer, as it turned out. I think of myself as "in remission." My genetic coding is fixed. Depression, for me, is cyclical and recurrent. If it returns, medication may stop it, and may not, but I know where to seek help and what works. That brings me to a wary acceptance of this condition, a fact of my life.

■